Teaching

The Troubled Child

Teaching
The Troubled Child

George T. Donahue, Ed.D.
and Sol Nichtern, M.D.

[Fp] THE FREE PRESS, NEW YORK
COLLIER-MACMILLAN LIMITED, LONDON

To the teacher-moms of Elmont, New York

The authors dedicate this book to all the
teacher-moms who made the Elmont project
possible. Because you have given a piece of
yourselves to children desperately in need, you
are an inspiration to the authors and to all the
professionals responsible for the education and
habilitation of Elmont's "different" children.
To you, and to all who follow, the authors are
grateful. So are the children and their parents
whom you help.

Acknowledgments

F OR the inspiration and stimulation that led to the establishment of the Elmont project, and for the case history material, the authors are indebted to school psychologists Mary Marans, Joan O'Shea, and Margaret Curtis. For some of the data in the chapter on the Community we are indebted to Doris Berryman. For the material concerning the education of the emotionally disturbed children and their progress we owe much to Madeline Dorn. Our manuscript typists were Frances Hopler, Betty Donahue, Josephine Taylor, and Miriam Gross.

To the teacher-moms who work daily with the children we are especially indebted:

Paula Albaum
Blanche Albin
Evelyn Armbruster
Helen Ayre
Reva Bach
Irene Berman
Audrey Bierman
Santina Bianco
Pearl Blank
Ethel Brody
Beverly Circharo
Fred Circharo
Blanche Cohen
Josephine D'Angelo
Bess Demos
Mildred Dickstein
Betty Donahue
Ida Drucker
Harriet Evans
Estelle Falk
Brenda Fishkow
Thelma Friedenthal
Sam Garfinkel
Helen Gerrard
Joyce Glaser

Nancy Gittings
Mary Ellen Hastry
Fran Hirx
Gwen Jacobs
Ethel Kadet
Rev. Duncan Kennedy
Phyllis Kreitzer
Bernice Lane
Sally LaPlaca
Joyce Leeds
Lillian Levenson
Sylvia Levin
Dolly Levine
Lois Lishkin
Nellie Lovstrom
Mollie Malinbaum
Renata Marini
Julia Nadler
Frieda Opperer
Beatrice Patterman
Sylvia Pergament
Irene Powell
Edna Ratcliffe
Lillian Ratner
Rose Ray

Kenneth Revell
Helen Richter
Selma Roachvarg
Shirley Roshevsky
Natalie Rubin
Selma Sachs
Muriel Safchick
Ethel Samenga
Janet Schumacher
Stuart Shein
Gloria Sherwyn
Gertrude Silver
Muriel Silver
Doree Smassenow
Norma Smooke
Helen Speier
Belle Steinberg
Ethel Steinberg
Sylvia Stewart
Sylvia Taylor
Bebe Toor
Gladys Weintraub
Esther Witner
Dorothy Strahs

We also wish to thank the Elmont Jewish Center for their generosity and cooperation; for medical direction we are indebted to Dr. Charles M. Brody.

Preface to the Paperback Edition

The twentieth century has been described frequently as the Century of the Child. Concern for their welfare has permeated all phases of our national life. Yet when we examine what is being done for our troubled children—children with defect, damage or disturbance—large gaps in necessary services can still be identified. A national concern with this problem prompted the Eighty-Ninth Congress of the United States to establish a Joint Commission on Mental Health of Children with the charge of developing "a program of research into and study of our resources, methods and procedures for diagnosing and preventing emotional illness in children, and of treating, caring for, and rehabilitating children with emotional illness." This mandate was the natural outgrowth of our country's awareness of the increasing and changing nature of the problems of our children. Not only has population burgeoned—doubling itself in the last forty years—but age distribution has shifted so that there are now more of the very young. Forty per cent of our total population is under twenty-one years of age, making a total of almost 80,000,000 individuals. Contrast this to the turn of the century when there were less than 75,000,000 people of all ages in our country. Our child-rearing practices have changed. The nature and composition of family life have been altered. The community and its organized structure has undergone an accelerating change. Thus, many values and traditions have disintegrated without adequate time or personnel available for the compensatory development of new systems. Locked into this change, with poor equipment to handle the accompanying stresses, many of our children have floundered and been cast adrift. Many of them have become victims of inadequate facilities, lack of programs and manpower shortages.

There is little question that our school system has been plagued by all of these problems. There is even less question that disturbed children have been devastated by the accompanying inadequacies. Faced with the overwhelming responsibility of providing a mass educational program for children whose numbers have increased more rapidly than the educational plant and its supply of manpower, the educator has had to resort to exclusion of children presenting problems. This policy of exclusion has resulted in hundreds of thousands of children becoming sidetracked and frequently having their disturbance accentuated by their isolation. Our greater devotion to our young has been accompanied by greater deficiencies in service to them. This contradiction has been the primary motivation in stimulating the demand for research and experimentation with new models for care and service. The Elmont Project, as the effort described in this book has become known, came into being as a direct response to the demands for new methods and practices. In retrospect, the real credit for the origin of this program must go to the children who demanded its creation through their disturbance and to the many different members of the community who expressed their devotion to children by supporting the initial efforts of the involved professionals. Also in retrospect, the readiness of the community to accept innovation and trial and error problem-solving were critical determinants in making this program successful.

Nine years after the inception of the Elmont Project, many changes have occurred. The six children who started in the program have long since gone from the school district. Some have moved on to successful living. Others have remained locked in their disturbance. Now the special project services as many as nineteen emotionally handicapped children at one time. This increase in number is not related to an increase in disturbance amongst the children. Rather, it reflects a better process of early identification and greater resources within the school district.

The original group of devoted teacher-moms has been enlarged by a much larger corps of women from the community. They function in the same model but are used not only with the project children but also with many other youngsters having difficulty in school. A variety of intermediate, transitional programs involving the teacher-moms has been made possible by a growing acceptance of their presence by the faculties of the schools and a willingness to experiment with new uses of these para-professionals.

There are now three groupings within the project itself. One is for five year-olds and less mature older children, numbering about six. These are with a certified school teacher and teacher-moms in a nursery-kindergarten atmosphere. These children are on a half-day schedule comparable to the original program.

The balance of the children come all day, five days a week and meet with another certified teacher in a very large classroom that has five small teaching cubicles along one wall, each approximately six by eight feet. The cubicles have a window portion, shelves, a pupil desk and chair, a teacher's chair, and colorful walls for the students to decorate with their work. A clock is provided in each cubicle for the accurate programming planned by the professional staff. While the younger children, ages seven to eight, work with the teacher for about half the morning, the older children, ages nine to eleven, work in the cubicles with teacher-moms. The schedule is reversed at midmorning. Under the new arrangement, each teacher-mom has two children on each of the two days she assists. Each child's schedule is developed by the teacher in consultation with the mental health team. It is flexible and involves individualized instructional practices suited to the child. The teacher, in addition to working with the class, is convenient enough to give not only special initial directions to the teacher-moms, but also can, in the course of group instruction, keep a watchful eye on the cubicles. The morning is broken up by a snack time. At noon the children have lunch in the school cafeteria and have a free play period mingling with all the other children in the school. In the afternoon, the project children are again separated down into small groups and spend periods of time with special subject teachers within the school, i.e., art, music, library, and physical education. Based on the progress of the child, he may be moved into a regular classroom for the afternoon with the accompanying presence and support of a teacher-mom. The morning teacher who has no group in the afternoon assists with half of the afternoon group. There is still a teacher coordinator for the entire program.

Many of the changes were made possible by the availability of space in one of the school buildings. This provided the long awaited opportunity to bring the special project into the mainstream of the school system. It immediately permitted greater utilization of existing resources of the school plant and personnel and the evolution of many more transitional programs.

It is important to re-emphasize the dramatic contribution of the small initial program to the life of the Elmont community. As a way was found to help these troubled children, a new attitude of acceptance grew and permeated many other areas of the community's relationship to its young and its disturbed. The concept of adaptation to the needs of the individual child grew and influenced the entire educational program of the school district. There had always been a heightened attitude of responsibility to children. However, the success of this program intensified the sensitivity to needs to such a degree that the principal benefactors of this special program became the majority of children within the school district.

At this time the principles of individualization and adaptation have been built into many programs throughout the country. Some of them have been modelled after the Elmont Project. Others have been motivated by similar circumstances to find a solution for their disturbed youngsters within the confines and resources of their own community structure. More and more communities are mobilizing their resources towards solving the problems presented by their children. As they do this the entire community seems to benefit.

The Elmont Project raises a number of serious questions. It postulates a broadened public school responsibility in the belief that there is therapeutic value in the educational process. It assumes that the resources to discharge this responsibility exists within the present structure of the educational system in conjunction with community effort and professional planning. It poses the issues of the critical need for reduction of class size and individualization and adaptation of educational programming. This might curtail the need for so much remediation. Is not the school the place for early identification and interference with processes destructive to normal development? The highly trained professionals, in short supply, must do as much of their work as possible through other professionals in greater supply and through para-professionals and responsible members of the community.

The Elmont Project through its original efforts demonstrated that most communities, given proper leadership, have the resources to solve many of their own problems. Now, nine years after its inception, this project is demonstrating that such self-help solutions can play a vital role in community life and have the energy for sustained growth.

Dr. George T. Donahue
Dr. Sol Nichtern

January 1968

Contents

xv

Teaching
The Troubled Child

1 The Troubled Child

CHILDREN are conceived, born and grow—the product of the nurturing ingredients of life, love, acceptance, and parental devotion. Introduce a disturbance—of conception (congenital defect), of birth (brain damage), or of growth (personality disturbance)—and more of these nurturing ingredients are needed. Combine some of these disturbances and extraordinary nurturing effort is required: effort which is not, unfortunately, always made. Too often the defect, or damage, or disturbance, breeds anxiety, rejection, isolation—and further disturbance. And so a destructive cycle is initiated. The victims, between 1 and 3 per cent of our children, now number in the millions. As they proceed through life, they must hurdle one barrier after another. They must survive physically, and they do, in spite of the many hazards which plague the young.

1

They must find love and devotion within their families, despite the many problems which complicate contemporary familial relationships. Finally, they must struggle to secure the acceptance of society and society's willingness to train and educate them, if they are to survive in the modern world.

It is here that we permit more than half a million of our children to fail. As a result of their difficulties they are excluded from school, rejected and isolated from their peers, and permitted to be victimized by their own lack of organization and order. These are our troubled children. They are the great challenge. If a way can be found to provide acceptance instead of rejection, if they can be included instead of isolated, and if their anxiety and disorganization can be allayed, we shall achieve a condition in which all of our children—and, as the children mature, our society—will flourish.

Empathy for these children can work miracles. Without it, they have difficulty surviving and functioning. But powerful as empathy is, fear and anxiety are equally powerful, in a destructive way. They can disrupt meaningful communication, chill the climate for adequate growth, and introduce a sense of hopelessness which may affect parents and all of us. The resultant apathy may make it almost impossible for parents to get meaningful help for these children and even more difficult to get any kind of education for them.

Fear and anxiety in five hundred thousand children— enough to make them so unacceptable that society thinks of them as children to be isolated, institutionalized, or hospitalized. How can this be, when these children have intelligence and are sometimes even brilliant? It is because they are considered seriously emotionally disturbed. Their world is different. It is a fearsome place of darkness, noise, threatening adults, threatening things; even their sleep, in many instances, is no release, because they suffer from nightmares. In some of these children, consequently, the motors run continually. There is sometimes a total disorganization of their ability to adapt and function. They defend themselves by striking out at other people and things—or at themselves, or by preserving their immaturity. Sometimes they refuse to learn. Their behavior is bizarre. They retreat into themselves. They may be anti-social and aggressive. Some refuse to acquire speech or hearing. Others perseverate—repeat the same things over and over. Some are unable or unwilling to sustain any effort. Others are uncontrollably impulsive, or sometimes frighteningly compulsive. Not all of such children have all of these symptoms, but all have some.

It is not possible for these children to learn in the normal public school classroom. Picture the impact on the learning process of the child who, unable to sit still, is in constant motion, or is preoccupied with incessant fiddling with a pencil or his crayons, or the buttons on his clothing. How can the child take visual or auditory instruction when he is hiding under his desk or in the cloak room; how can his opposite, who runs around and around the room, or climbs over the desk? How can a child be receptive to a reading lesson when he persists in making animal noises, or imitating the tic toc of a clock, or perseverating the arithmetic problems of the previous lesson? How much can a child learn when he is screaming, or striking out at his neighbors? How can a child learn when, because he is lashing out or kicking out, he is rejected by the teacher and the other children? When one youngster insists on making animal noises, can he, or the other thirty children in the class, be taught anything? What can a child learn who is persistently a clown, or a dog, or a tiger, or a rocket in space, or anything except an attentive member of the class? How can a child who will not speak or hear respond to a reading lesson? How can a child accept the reality and limits of an arithmetic lesson whose fantasy has him in outer space, or in an awesome monster-universe, or in a world of friendly, accepting animals? How much can a child learn whose attention span is fragmented into seconds and minutes?

And what of the child who cannot take care of his creature needs, or who soils himself in the classroom?

Are they hopeless? One would think so, to judge by the puny efforts being made to help them. But they are far from hopeless. They can be stuck together. They can be educated —and that is what this book is about. It can be done when the educator, the psychologist, and the psychiatrist team up; and when the community mobilizes its resources to help—not with money, but with space, people, and schools. The welding of these professional and community resources into a structure to accommodate these children can provide the nurture and empathy for their growth and learning. The experience of Elmont, New York, bears this out.

The story begins in 1959, at a meeting of three school psychologists in the office of the school administrator—one of the co-authors. Six seriously disturbed children had been identified, who, during the year, had to be excluded from school because they could not adjust to the group setting in the classrooms. The school psychologists had made the identification, and together with the school's medical personnel and the consulting psychiatrist (one of the co-authors), had agreed on diagnoses and analyses of the family relationships. Their purpose in meeting with the school administrator was to request that the school system provide an educational program adapted to the needs of these children.

The school psychologist's interest in children as individuals is one reason why all school districts should have access to psychological services. School administration deals in numbers and groups; often the needs of individual children will be overlooked if there is no one on the staff with responsibility for them. This is one of the functions of the school psychologist; therefore the three had come to the office of the assistant to the superintendent. They indicated to him their belief that it was the duty of the system to provide appropriate education for these disturbed children.

But what kind of program? For many weeks discussions went forward during which the psychologists described the needs of these children and the kinds of adaptations required. There were few, if any, guideposts in the professional literature. There was much on techniques for identification, but the literature provided scanty information about how to work with these children. Here too the school psychologists were most helpful. They discussed with the educational administrator the symptomatology of the children, and he was able to identify the ingredients needed for programing. If the children were distractible then distractibility would have to be reduced to a minimum. This meant no more than two to a room. Children who were unpredictable and subject to extreme mood swings would need total flexibility in programing. Fear and anxiety, insecurity, hyperactivity, intrinsic personality distortions, often complicated by segregation and isolation and occasionally by lack of parental understanding, strongly suggested the need for a one-to-one empathic teaching relationship.

The answer was simple and revolutionary. The school system would recruit a corps of women successful in their own child-rearing practices, as evidenced by their own healthy children. These mothers would be added as a fourth member to the team of educator, psychologist, psychiatrist. Thus the nonprofessional would become a part of, and an extension of, the professionally trained team. Her responsibility would be to conduct the educational and emotional program as prescribed by the professional members of the team and under their sustained direction and supervision. Space was requested and secured free of charge from the Elmont Jewish Center. Transportation, books, supplies, a highly qualified teacher-in-charge, psychological, psychiatric, and medical supervision, were provided by the Elmont Board of Education. The Elmont Kiwanis Club was asked to underwrite any extraordinary expenditures and quickly agreed. People, space, and schools were at hand, and the program was under way: a total community effort to attack, at the local level, a nationwide problem. What follows tells in detail about this effort, its results, and its implications.

The public schoolman believes his function is to educate all the educable children of all the people. Troubled children too can be educated, and in the process develop enough integration of personality to become like all children—able to take their place in the regular school, happy with their peers, learning and developing.

There are good reasons why we should help these children and their parents. One is the Judaeo-Christian ethic of charity: not with money but with sharing of oneself—*caritas*. It is this, and in large quantities, that is needed. Love for neighbor—and these children and their parents are our neighbors. It is the basis of most of our religions. Given freely to some of the most difficult of all children in the world to love, it is a practical expression of what we profess to believe. Working with these children requires from everyone concerned—the educator, the psychologist, the psychiatrist, medical people—a piece of himself, not money. For the people involved who give of themselves and their skills, there are few tangible rewards. But they will tell you that their reward is the satisfaction of seeing a sick child begin to get well and to learn. It gives them a meaningful purpose, a creative outlet for their energies, and makes them feel a part of a heroic effort: the creation of a functioning human being. And this is a very great satisfaction, as all school people and others working with children will agree.

There are some selfish reasons, too, why communities should try to help. These half-million children, and there are more born every year, represent an appalling waste of our human resources. This at a time when every human talent the nation possesses needs to be developed to the fullest extent possible. As President Eisenhower pointed out, "Education is second in importance only to national defense." Or, as Nikita

Khrushchev said when he was in New York: "We train ten times as many engineers as you. He who has the education has the power." Later you will meet Steve, a little fellow unable to defend himself against his environment and his own vulnerability, who is literally at the genius level in mathematics and science. The nation cannot afford the profligacy of wasting people of this capability: there are only one or two born in every hundred children.

The prognosis generally for these children is either hospitalization or institutionalization. If they are helped early there will be a preventive value in terms of the nation's mental health problem. If mentally ill children can be found and helped it should reduce, in part, the number of mentally ill adults. Rashi Fein estimates the direct costs of mental illness in the United States to be about $1.7 billion.[1] He estimates indirect costs at approximately $3.5 billion, just for those institutionalized and hospitalized in public institutions. The cost for those in private care and at community mental health centers is impossible to estimate accurately but is probably equally large, if not larger.

Looking at the problem from the more important viewpoint of the numbers of people involved, some startling data have been published. Mental health authorities point out that in addition to the half-million seriously mentally ill children who are the subject of this book, probably 5 to 10 per cent of the nation's school children are sufficiently upset to require professional help. If this estimate is reasonable (it probably is, since some authorities estimate as high as 50 per cent), then another four million children are involved for whom, in many communities, little is being done. It is no wonder then that mental illness is the chief medical problem in the United States.

Perhaps a good way to grasp the scope of the problem is

1. Fein, Rashi, *Economics of Mental Illness.* Basic Books, New York, 1958.

to look at some of the dramatic statistics commonly quoted, and emphasized in *Action for Mental Health*.[2] This report says that nearly half of all the hospital beds in the United States are occupied by mental patients, that there are almost seven hundred thousand patients of all types at any given time; that probably seventeen million persons suffer from some kind of mental disturbance or mental illness. In New York State, hospital custodial care costs about $1,800 per year per patient—officially. There is one report that indicates that for children in one hospital, the cost to the taxpayers is actually almost $3,500. Considered selfishly, any program that might make inroads on the numbers of mentally ill, and do it at reasonable cost, would be a prudent community expenditure. The Elmont program costs about $670 per ·pupil—about what is spent on normal students. But more about this later.

How are these children, the half-million, handled now? One of the most heartbreaking experiences is to listen to a story related by parents of a seriously disturbed child. Often the pattern runs something like this: By age one the mother has begun to observe that the child does not turn, or make sounds, or try to crawl or walk, as do her friends' children. "He hardly cries, just lies in the crib . . . never demands anything . . . he's a good baby." Or the child constantly screams, rocks, and bangs his head. At this point the husband and wife anxiously discuss the child's behavior. The husband tries to reassure the mother, and for another period of time they tolerate the situation and try to avoid discussing it. Then one day the mother again talks to the father and he agrees, because it has been gnawing at him too, that they ought to go to the doctor—often a pediatrician. The doctor, in turn, reacts in one of two ways. Because the child appears physically well he advises, "Don't worry, he'll grow out of it, give him time," which, of course, does not happen. The child goes from bad to

2. *Action for Mental Health: Final Report of the Joint Commission on Mental Illness and Health.* Basic Books, New York, 1961.

worse. Or he advises the parents, "I can't find anything wrong
with him, but I'd like you to have some tests completed." So
a referral is made to a neurologist. The neurologist tests for
signs of brain damage or damage to the central nervous system.
But the level of sophistication of medical science, unfortunately, is not so high that results are always conclusive. In
many instances the neurologist can identify nothing specific,
and so the parents struggle along for another period of time.
Meanwhile the child is getting older, and his behavior is becoming more clearly atypical. Perhaps, during this period, the
parents try another doctor or two about whom they have
heard from friends or relatives, frustrated meanwhile because
not only is no illness being pinned down, but because they
are getting little or no real advice or direction. This is a critical
matter at this point, because if the child is mishandled the
basic problem will only be aggravated.

The bills are mounting. This makes for more problems.
Sometimes the father blames the mother, saying something
like, "What are you doing to this child when I'm not around
that makes him this way?" Then he takes over—from one
doctor to another, and so on. If there are other children in the
family they too suffer because all the psychic energy of the
parents is being expended on the "different" child. The whole
family structure and routine is geared to accommodate the
"baby." Then the school calls and says it can't understand
what is happening. One of the older children is acting-out, aggressive, hostile. The parents can't understand either: "He's
so helpful with his little brother."

Finally, after several years, the parents get to a good
hospital clinic staffed with a full complement of medical,
psychological and psychiatric disciplines, and the diagnosis is
made. Your child is schizophrenic or brain damaged—or seriously emotionally disturbed. Competent advice is given to the
parents on how to handle the child and (hopefully) the other
children in the family.

The child has now reached school age and the hospital staff tells the parents that he'll need special educational programing. The chances are, unless the parents are wealthy, little or nothing is available to them. But it takes them a while to find this out, while they suffer another series of frustrating and sometimes humiliating experiences, as public and private educational doors are slammed in their faces. It's true the state hospital is available, or private facilities, if they can get on the waiting list or if they can afford anything from $2,500 to $20,000 a year. These facilities exist and many are doing a creditable job. But there are not enough of them and most cannot accommodate children of parents of average means.

Fortunate, in a way, are the parents who go to a pediatrician or family doctor who is oriented to children's emotional problems. He promptly arranges either for a hospital clinic workup on the child, or coordinates a private workup by psychologist, neurologist, psychiatrist, and such others— otologist, ophthalmologist—as are needed. These parents are advised that the youngster is a childhood schizophrenic, and/or brain damaged, and/or seriously emotionally disturbed. Often, however, the parents are not ready to accept this, and go the rounds from one psychologist to another, one psychiatrist to another, one neurologist to another. Or, if they are agency savvy, from one agency to another.

Another group of parents is represented by a child who will be discussed later in this book, an autistic, aphasic child. She was withdrawn, with no usable speech, and was known literally to every speech and hearing clinic in a large neighboring city. None of these were able to help because the basic problem was not lack of speech, but lack of speech because of emotional illness. More often than not, parents with a child such as she struggle along until the child reaches school age. At this time she is either admitted and shortly exempted from school, or the parents are advised to find special educational programing. Special programing is either nonexistent or too costly, or available only in a state hospital, which the parents are not ready to accept.

There is a third group of parents who, for whatever reason, do nothing to try to identify the trouble. At age five they bring him to school to register. During the pre-school period, it frequently emerges, they had treated the child inconsistently, alternating strict discipline, isolation, sometimes physical punishment, with complete permissiveness. This behavior sometimes aggravates the basic illness. The child is registered and, if he is an acting-out child, quickly identified by the school as atypical and incapable of being managed in the normal group setting. He is exempted from school attendance. Sometimes he is placed on home teaching until he grows too big to handle. He may then be hospitalized and some help given, or at least placed in an environment which is understanding if not habilitative. The prognosis by then is poor, and the child may become a ward of the state indefinitely.

The most unfortunate child, however, is the withdrawn or autistic child who may go unnoticed for a number of years by the school people. He is usually little trouble to himself, the teachers, or the other children. One day, somehow or other, he can go no further, and he too is excluded. Often, sadly, he is hospitalized with the same discouraging prognosis.

What of the child who is institutionalized? As residential treatment facilities function in this country, very often, although not always, a host of other problems develop.

The institutionalized child is exposed to the problem of separation anxiety. This is usually a disruptive force in the inner life of the emotionally immature or disturbed child, and his anxiety serves to stimulate the very defenses which constitute his pathology. Thus hyperactivity, withdrawal, regression, destructive or impulsive behavior, increased fantasy, sleep and eating problems, may be seen in the initial stages of his commitment to an institution. Depending upon the degree of disturbance this may last for a considerable time.

Although it eventually subsides as the child adapts to his new environment, the same thing frequently occurs, in the vulnerable child, when attempts are made to move him back into the community.

Disruption of normal group relations invariably takes place when children are moved into a program of institutional care. Residential units, because of their organization, require that children be grouped according to age, sex, and the nature of their problems, as well as according to the level of what is measured as "intelligence." This kind of grouping is actually motivated by convenience of administration, not the needs of the child. It obviously disrupts a normal, spontaneous grouping, which would emerge within the community and among peers. It frequently represents an artificiality which is not duplicated in normal society. As a result, children coming from long term institutional care have great difficulty in adjusting, when they return, to their home community.

Artificial institutional grouping often leads to anti-social practices. Homosexuality is a common practice spawned in institutions and widely known, but rarely mentioned and seldom, if ever, treated. A peer hierarchy, which bears little resemblance to the spontaneous pattern within the normal community, frequently emerges. An attitude toward authority may develop in which authority is viewed purely as a restrictive and confining force, to be constantly challenged and tested.

A policy of segregation occurs in many residential units as a consequence of administration, origin or financing of the facility, or the attitude of the professional staff in its intake. This policy may extend into every area, including diagnostic concepts. The result is exposure of the child to an experience dedicated to a subtle kind of segregation, which reaches into the many practices and structures of his community.

It must be remembered that these children compose the most vulnerable and impressionable segment of society. They frequently reflect the pathology of their families and of society in their own personal makeup; thus the acting-out of the emotionally disturbed youngster often reveals the established patterns of delinquency within the community. This may operate within the residential facility as well.

Just as within the community there is a hierarchy which emerges for social organization, so also does it occur within the institution. A pecking order develops. Within the residential unit, this pecking order is an artificial one. Rarely does it approximate the natural or desirable social organization which evolves within most communities. Children who become the long term product of institutional care develop values and morality which bear little resemblance to those of children reared within the community.

When these problems are considered, it must be remembered why institutions originally came into existence. For the most part, they represented solutions by the existing culture to deal with individuals who appeared to be incompatible with the organization of society. As the concept of institutionalization developed, it began to be universally applied to solve problems. In time, it became acceptable. Some of society's devices, however, do not necessarily merit universal application. Society evolves to new and different forms. The necessity to adapt society to the needs of the individual is a part of the thesis of this book as it applies specifically to the educational system. Many children are excluded not because it is to their benefit to be excluded, but because it is an accepted policy and a pattern of problem solving; and because the tendency is to isolate extremes. The price society pays is a growing conformity.

Children who have been institutionalized with severe emotional problems tend, by definition, to remain in isolation. Their return to family and community becomes more and more difficult to achieve. One problem that plagues many residential facilities is the reluctance or inability of the community to take back the child who is ready to be returned to it. Children are sometimes maintained within residential facilities long after their placement has served any useful purpose. Sometimes the point is reached where all the positive gains achieved by such placement are dissipated. A new series of problems associated with chronic institutional care are then substituted, which can sometimes be more serious than the original set that brought the child there in the first place.

The imprinting process of long term institutional care is known to most professionals who have worked in this area. One problem it creates for the children is chronic dependency on the authority figure. Institutional values seem to take priority over community values. Isolation from the community and its organized systems can occur. This substitution of the organized system of the institution can result in emotional isolation from family values, which reflect the basic unit of society.

On the other hand, it is important to stress that the institution has certain specific values when used appropriately, and to meet specific needs. It does provide structured living for children who are extremely unstructured. It sometimes serves to interrupt disruptive reactive processes within the child, or between the child and his family, or between the child and the community. It must be recognized that there is a need for such facilities in the care of the emotionally disturbed child—but they should not be used by society to solve its own problems. Their function should be to solve the problems of the child.

The use of the residential unit sometimes serves to reduce stresses on the child. Living becomes simplified into living with the world of peers. Pressures to conform to the demands of a complex society are reduced. Responsibility for decisions is minimized. In the child who is being overwhelmed for the moment by his inability to cope successfully with his environment, the residential unit has much to offer. Still, it must be repeated that the residential facility should be a unit designed to meet the specific needs of the child, not the needs of the community.

Another problem of institutional care is the separation of the family from the problems of the child, eliminating the need for the family to help solve these problems. As long as society is organized around the family as the primary child-rearing unit, the introduction of an alternative solution for child-rearing poses many problems to the family as well as the child. Once the child is removed the family restructures itself and develops new patterns with the child eliminated. This may account, in part, for the many difficulties encountered in returning a child to his family. The family may have so re-organized itself that it chooses not to reinvest itself in his problems. This will make it impossible for the child to return. Or, when he does return, the family may have difficulty in modifying its new structure to his needs. Or, having adapted itself to an equilibrium in which it is free of his problems, it may be unable to adapt to the child—who may have actually undergone change requiring a completely different family orientation.

In other instances, the elimination of the child permits the pathology within the family to remain untouched and thus hardened. The child's disturbed behavior is sometimes a reaction to intra-family difficulties and his reactive process prevents the pathology from expanding. When the child is eliminated the disturbance within the family may extend into other areas, and ultimately serve to prevent the child from ever successfully returning to the family. It is interesting to note that, in some of the cases presented later, preserving the child within the family and instituting changes in the child ulti-mately resulted in some positive changes in the child-family relationship. On the other hand, in one instance, when a child was institutionalized and returned to the family within a very short space of time, the family found reason to reinstitutionalize him—even though experience with him in the Elmont project suggested he was very much improved.

Since many institutions have inadequate provisions for preparing the child or the family for his return, it is important that such programs be developed in recognition of the need to readjust both child and family to each other.

In some other countries of the world, approaches other than institutional care as structured in the United States have been tried, and with some degree of success. Included among these is the program of Youth Aliyah in Israel. This organization was spawned by a dozen Jewish boys who asked a German Zionist leader, Recha Freirer, to help them after they had lost their jobs in Berlin in 1932. Mrs. Freier had the inspiration to suggest that these boys consider going to Israel, settle on the soil, and perhaps resolve their own economic problems while also assisting Israel.

Hitler came to power in January, 1933. Farsighted Jews began to make plans, particularly for their children. As Hitler moved to destroy European Jewry, Youth Aliyah, the youth-saving organization of Israel, took care of thousands of new children yearly. It recently took in its hundred-thousandth child. In addition to the European children, others began to pour in from North Africa and the East.

Henrietta Szold was given the task of developing Youth Aliyah. She evolved a basic two-year program of education and, more important, she imprinted her own characteristics of motherliness and abiding love on this organization for displaced youth. She met every child that came in and succeeded in creating an organization that, of necessity, dealt with masses of children, but with each child as an individual.

Many of these children were without parents, relations, or friends in Israel. Because of their experiences they had severe emotional overlays. She organized them into groups to provide a social base as a kind of substitute for their lost family life, and developed an education program which, together with work on

the land, transformed these young people into goal-oriented
and productive citizens. They lived in hundreds of relatively
small settlements throughout Israel. Their leaders were the
madrichim, or teachers. These were generally non-professionals, trained in short term programs by Youth Aliyah. As-
sisted by the support of the community women's Zionist
organization, Hadassah, professionals in the sciences of medicine, psychology and child guidance were added. Thus emerged
a program of help to youth, combining the resources and
talents of the community, plus the professionals.

The results have been most challenging. By its twenty-fifth
anniversary it had "rescued" ninety thousand children from
seventy-two countries and had made them useful and productive citizens of Israel.

The chief element, perhaps, is Henrietta Szold—"motherliness and abiding love"—followed by the contribution of education, medicine, psychology, social work and psychiatry; and
finally, productive and useful work: all three applied simultaneously.

Another approach to the problems of the troubled child
is seen in some of the Eastern cultures, where the emotionally
disturbed individual is viewed as being "touched by the hand
of God." This leads to the fundamental moral attitude that
all such individuals are the responsibility of every member of
the community. The emotionally disturbed person then, is
seldom, if ever, isolated from his home community. With this
moral commitment of the community to his welfare, only
those who are a danger to themselves or to the physical safety
of others are ever institutionalized. This points up the need
for an acceptance of responsibility on the part of communities.

The Elmont program is a fusion of the elements of acceptance of responsibility by the community; the team approach of educator, psychologist, psychiatrist and social worker;
plus "motherliness and abiding love."

2 Education and the Troubled Child

W H Y isn't more being done for the troubled child, particularly by our schools? It is not because school people are unsympathetic. It is because we are making impossible demands on school people, without providing real support of education even for the normal child, let alone the deviant, emotionally disturbed child. It is because there is a tradition of exclusion and institutionalization, with which schoolmen have grown up. And it is because little is known about how to deal with, and educate, the emotionally disturbed child.

Then there is the nature of the children themselves. These are perhaps the most difficult of all children and, therefore, as a group lack the appeal most other children have. They frequently withdraw from proffered help or reject it outright. As a result, those in a position to help react themselves by

19

rejecting the child. By so doing they aggravate the original condition and the child becomes more ill than he was before.

It seems appropriate, therefore, to take a look at what the country's educators confront. If the thesis of this book is accepted—that schools have to accept a large share of the job of educating the emotionally disturbed child—it is important to understand what will be necessary. It is important to look at these problems, because they have an impact on the emerging philosophy of public education.

It is commonly accepted by most people that the job of the public schools is to provide an education for all the children of all the people. This will enable each child to develop his capacity to the fullest extent possible, so that the child becomes a self-sustaining, contributing, and self-fulfilled member of society. There are some, of course, who do not accept all of this philosophy. Some accept none of it. But in general, people, and particularly parents, want education at public expense adapted to the needs and capacities of all children. This is becoming increasingly difficult to provide, because for some reason the people of this country have never supported education in proportion to what they ask the public schools to do.

Some facts published in the *National Education Research Bulletin* will help put the problem in perspective. The year 1960–61 is used to permit some comparisons with the decade 1950–60. The bulletin indicates that the school age population during that ten-year period increased 47 per cent, from 30,730,-000 in July, 1950, to 45,044,000 in July, 1960. Enrollments increased at a rate of more than a million students per year. For the one-year period 1960–61, as contrasted with 1959–60, the bulletin points out:

Pupil enrollment: 37,244,284—up 3.3 per cent from 1959–60. Instructional staff: 1,526,079—up 4. 2 per cent from 1959–60. Classroom teachers: 1,408,962—up 4.2 per cent from 1959–60. Instructional staff average salary: $5,389—up 4.5 per cent from 1959-60. Revenue receipts: $14,778,972,000—up 7.7 per cent from 1959-60. Current expense: $12,929,564,000—up 8.3 per cent from 1959-60. Capital outlay: $3,094,621,000—up 5.4 per cent from 1959-60. Current expense per pupil in average daily attendance: $390—up 4.8 per cent from 1959-60.

As of September, 1960, 110,000 teachers were needed to replace those leaving the profession the year before; 30,000 to serve increased enrollments; 30,000 to relieve overcrowding and half-day sessions: 20,000 to give instruction and services not now provided; and 40,000 to replace the unprepared—a total of 230,000.[1]

Most people will readily agree that keeping up with the sheer weight of this enormous growth was a staggering problem. To provide buildings, staffs, and instructional materials is itself a herculean task for boards of education and professional schoolmen. This could well have taxed their energies to the point that little was left over for some of the other problems that were to emerge or become emphatic during that decade. For instance: (1) The problem of the bright or talented student. (2) The problem of the high school dropout or pushout. (3) The problem of improving the quality of education in response to the demands of our times. (4) The problem of the disadvantaged and the delinquent. (5) The problem of social segregation. (6) The problem of all categories of the handicapped other than the emotionally disturbed (who are generally overlooked). And there are others.

The same N. E. A. bulletin, in the section "How the States Compare on School Support," reads as follows:

Public Education is one of the most important jobs for which the states are responsible. On the efficiency with which it is done depends our national security, our economic independence and much of the quality of our citizens.

About 21 per cent of the total population is enrolled in public elementary and secondary schools.

1. *National Education Research Bulletin*, Vol. XXXIX, No. 1 (February, 1961).

In the main, public schools are supported by taxes paid out of the personal income of the people of the respective states. In Delaware, the total income of persons in the state divided by the number of pupils enrolled is $15,984; in Mississippi, it is $4,397.

For the 37.2 million pupils enrolled in public elementary and secondary schools in 1960–61, the nation is paying a bill of $13 billion, or $390 for every pupil attending, for current expenses exclusive of interest and new buildings. Some states spend more— Alaska, New York, and New Jersey, more than $500 per pupil; other states, much less—Alabama and South Carolina, less than $225 per pupil. . . . The rank in expenditures . . . tends to be similar to the rank in resources. . . .

The cost of educating each child increased during the past 10 years partly because of inflation. But most states have also improved the quality of education. Mississippi's expenditure in 1960–61 was 142.9 per cent greater than in 1950–51; Nebraska's only 36.2 per cent. . . .

Differences in salaries of teachers tend to reflect differences in the quality of instruction that pupils receive. The average salary paid classroom teachers in 1960–61 was estimated at $5,215. Teachers in California, Alaska, and New York are paid, on the average, more than $6,000, and teachers in South Dakota, Arkansas, and Mississippi, less than $3,700. . . .[2]

In short, spending for public education amounted to about 10 per cent of all governmental expenditures. If education is second in importance only to national defense, then there is a wide gap between the roughly $50 billion spent for national defense in 1960 and the $15 billion spent for public education. It is apparent that the problems of public education are tremendous, whereas financial support leaves something to be desired. No wonder that the schools have been able to do so little for disturbed children.

Turning to the programs of the schools and their organization, here, too, are some built-in problems that militate against help for the troubled.

Public education is of necessity a group process, because no

2. Ibid.

community could possibly afford the ideal of one teacher to
one pupil. The system of grouping children by age, by grade,
and later by course choice or trends, such as vocational,
academic, or business, has worked reasonably well in this
country in one respect. It has helped develop the best fed,
strongest, most affluent nation the world has ever seen. It has
aided in moving the economy from a point where 90 per cent
of the people once had to be engaged in providing the food
and fibers to our present circumstance, where 10 per cent of
the people do the same work better quantitatively and qualita-
tively, and, in the process, create staggering agricultural
surpluses. It has helped develop the intellectual and physical
resources that make the United States the leader of the free
world and a substantial supporter of large sections of that
world. It has made possible the doubling of scientific knowledge every ten years—and has resulted in a culture in which
90 per cent of all the scientists who ever lived are alive now.

And yet, despite this amazing record of achievement,
schoolmen are concerned. Recently the American Association
of School Administrators; the Association for Supervision and
Curriculum Development; the National Association of Secondary School Principals; the National Education Association,
Department of Elementary School Principals; and the National Education Association, Department of Rural Education
jointly issued a pamphlet: *Labels and Fingerprints.* The point
of this joint statement centers around a real concern that education is moving in a direction, as is our society, that tends to
ignore the individual. All of the pamphlet is worth quoting, but
here are two pertinent excerpts:

The individual is as unique as his fingerprints. Even a label
cannot obscure his individuality. He may be a Kansan or a Cali-
fornian, but these names do not describe him. So it is with all
labels. But the fingerprint is unmistakably individual—always
symbolic of the uniqueness of every personality.

Basically, life is individual. A child is born, grows up, goes to school, makes a living, marries, finds a house or apartment, rears his children, gradually gets older, and, when the time comes, dies. All along, the erstwhile child thinks, talks, eats, sleeps; represents himself to the other people in the world, and struggles with his environment.

How does man or woman go through all these experiences of life? As an individual? By himself? Of course. The universe insists that a child, himself, be born, and a man, himself, die. No one can inhabit his body; no one can live and die for him.

Now what has all this to do with education? If values are kept straight, it has everything to do with it. And that is what *Labels and Fingerprints* is about.

The signs today are ominous. The heritage that America has so well guarded, full personal development in ways most suited to each man's nature—this heritage now is threatened; and when the individual is threatened, our democratic society is in danger. The danger becomes more acute when the teaching profession is under pressure from many directions to bypass its obligations to the individual child, or when it deserts its own responsibility and high purpose.

Are we retreating from that ideal which has made American citizenship the envy of much of the world? Are we drifting away from making the dignity and inherent worth of the individual person pre-eminent among our values?

It is not in the might of the military, the productivity of industry, or the efficiency of transportation and communication that the true greatness of America lies. Rather, it is in the high esteem accorded the individual personality. Here, indeed, is our greatest contribution to men everywhere, and here is America's greatest secret weapon. Our philosophy of government from its very beginning, our deepest convictions, and our highest ideals have sought to clothe the individual with a sense of dignity, to recognize his potentialities, to unloose his creative powers, and to stimulate his initiative. It was on this platform that Jefferson, Adams, Lincoln, and Wilson rose to greatness.

And yet, despite these fundamental concepts and ideas, we seem to be drifting toward impersonality in almost every sphere of our culture. Individuality is tending to be submerged in gigantic organizations, in chain-belt production, in monolithic economic enterprise, and in the complex cultural interdependence of our society.

. . . .

Within the schools of America can be found dozens of practices and procedures which obscure the individual and promote the group pattern. Although many of these practices were originally designed to make teaching of the individual easier, they seldom have achieved the goal. In fact, by eliminating the obvious deviate, they sometimes obscure the differences which still remain.[3]

There are then, and always will be, some children who do not or will not fit the group mold. Among them are the seriously emotionally disturbed. They are sometimes the most obvious deviates, sometimes the least obvious of all and the most difficult to deal with. Yet this book demonstrates that these children can be educated within the community setting by public schools, and in the process develop a degree of emotional health that enables them to function there.

The public schools then, have a tremendous responsibility. They must be helped by all of us to discharge it. We can continue to exclude the deviate and build bigger and better hospitals and institutions—and we shall never catch up with the problem, let alone resolve it. It must be recognized that the public schools are the only institution in our culture large enough to cope with the enormousness of the task and with a large enough staff oriented to children and their development to make a major impact on the problem.

So it is with amazement that we listen to the proposals of some educators, and self-appointed educational experts, for our present schools as well as the hypothetical schools of the 1980's. There is, in fact, one group at a leading university presently structuring the school of the 1980's—as though we had resolved the problems of the school of the 1960's. What

3. *Labels and Fingerprints*. National Education Association, Washington, D.C., n.d. (1964).

we need is to come to grips with the educational crisis which is here now. A resolution of the present crisis would make a greater contribution to education in the 1980's than trying to peer into a crystal ball.

There are people, who have never worked with children or public school teachers, who suggest how to train teachers and recommend a reorganization of content and time-structure, while they overlook the great need for teachers with more background in the behavioral sciences. A constructor of submarines would have school people forget all but the gifted. Mechanically apt psychologists offer the teaching machine as the answer. Administrative technicians suggest homogeneous grouping, ungraded schools, team teaching, and programed texts as partial solutions. Not to be overlooked are the frustrated Madison Avenue mass communicators, promoting closed circuit television as the panacea. Transistor buffs suggest computers and data processing as a solution. A governor and a legislature promote good schools and better education as long as they don't cost money. Professional time and the taxpayer's money are being poured into administrative gadgets and gimmicks of dubious value, which may even be detrimental to the development of better education.

We are a nation of mass producers, of automated production of goods and services that are constantly changing. There is danger that we may apply the principles of production to the educational enterprise, which by its nature is a *people* operation. Children are *people*—despite what you read and hear from some newspaper columnists, magazine writers and radio commentators. If we continue in this direction, we're headed for disaster. We shall produce generations of automated automatons, instructed but not educated—automatically; reading in unison as predicted by a computer and taught by a machine via closed circuit television—and probably sick, sick, sick. The incidence of ulcers in young people is rapidly rising. So is the number of college suicides. The National

Institute of Mental Health and the National Mental Health Association have called attention to the rate of increase of mental illness in our children (adults, too). Perhaps these are signposts to our future that need to be thought about and interpreted by human beings, not computers.

The pressures on our young people are enormous, placed on them particularly by parents who want them to go to college. College is a status symbol and, presumably, the "open sesame" to life, liberty and the acquisition of happiness.

But some of our young people are not the right color, or in the right place, or there at the right time. The situation has not been helped by college admissions officers who take the easy way out by delegating their responsibilities to testing organizations that test everything except a child's ability to progress. They often test where the child has been rather than where he might go if given the chance. It is as though all children have been to the same places and develop at the same rate in the same way, like our mass produced goods. Here too, children are no longer people. They are test statistics, identified by a number code—even their names have been taken away. It is true that these tests do measure capacity in a limited way, but in a not-so-limited way what they really measure are variables, such as the child's developmental lags, the deficits in his education because of the quality or lack of it in the school program offered in his community, or the degree of cultural enrichment or lack thereof occasioned by the accident of his birth or color.

We may be losing sight of the fact that our children are human. They are not things to be machined, measured with calipers or Johansson blocks, quality controlled, mass produced, packaged, and merchandised at the end of the assembly line, alike in their components, performance and reactions. Maybe we'd better take a look at what we're doing, how we're doing it, and where we're headed, in our educational establishment.

The thoughtful educator—the one in an operational job, like a superintendent of schools, a principal, a teacher—who tries to provide for the educational needs of children now, knows that he has to deal with our children as children. He knows now and has known for a long while that his job is primarily one of human relationships, person to person. He knows now and has known that the key to unlocking the learning process is the relationship that exists between the child and the teacher. And it is precisely here that he needs help from the behavioral sciences. He's not apt to get it in the kind or quantity needed in the near future, because our research efforts and money are going into missiles, trips to the moon, automation, all designed to improve human relations, but probably by removing the need for relations.

Regardless of the level at which he works, the educator's job is one of identification and adaptation. He must identify the needs of children for whom he is responsible and then adapt the program to those needs. Too often, however, this is not what happens. A group mold is designed and developed and the children are stuffed into this preconceived mold and kneaded and prodded to fit it. This works for those who fit. But what of those who can't or won't? These are the ones who have to face a daily dose of failure. What child—or adult, for that matter—can long tolerate or survive a daily dose of failure? These are the discards, the pushouts, and maybe, eventually, the hopelessly unemployed or delinquent.

If improvement in the quality of education is to be made in this country, it is going to come through improved human relations in the classroom, and greater facility in identifying children's needs and adapting to them.

One of the more interesting dialogues going on at the moment in professional education circles has to do with teacher-training. The education professors have been feuding with the subject matter professors about whether or not method and technique are more important than knowledge of subject matter. Actually the winner is the state licensing authority, since it prescribes in detail what student teachers must complete in the way of content and methodology to be certified to teach. Entering the fray recently has been a former college president who probably hasn't taught in an elementary, junior high, or high school in the last generation. He advocates a longer internship for student teachers and thinks teacher certification should be the prerogative of the colleges and universities. He believes, too, that more emphasis should be placed on knowledge of subject matter. Competence in subject matter, however, does not make for competence in transmitting it to children.

All of these viewpoints have merit, although it would be disastrous to permit colleges and universities to become the certifying agencies. In fact, some of the worst teaching is done at the college level, and often by the very education professors who are supposed to be expert enough to teach others how to teach. It will be a sorry day for elementary and secondary children when their teachers teach by emulating the professors.

All of these groups are really tilting at windmills. Teachers who have been certified recently are pretty well prepared in subject matter and have relatively good backgrounds in methods and techniques. The three areas that need strengthening are, first, the selection procedures for admitting young people to teacher-training programs; second, the quantity and quality of courses they should be required to complete in child psychology and child development; and third, the choice of school systems in which they do their interning.

Educators, too, are concerned with such matters as providing adequate buildings and staffs to accommodate the population explosion, with inadequate funds, with the issues of kinds and amounts of general and vocational education in our times, and with a host of other matters. These, while important, sometimes serve to divert the attention of schoolmen from the basic issue: to structure a system that will identify the needs of individual children and adapt itself to those needs and to the needs of the community in its broad sense, as well as to the personnel employed in the whole educational enterprise.

It is into this background of education and this kind of controversy that programs for emotionally disturbed children have to be fitted. No wonder progress in programing for disturbed children has moved so slowly, and will continue to progress slowly. Educators have many other preoccupations, broader based than the problem of the minority of emotionally handicapped youngsters. Complicating the problem is the fact that not much is known about how to educate them.

Further confusing the situation are the current methods of handling these children. In brief, the children are usually excluded from school and eventually institutionalized, or hospitalized as wards of the state. Why do we do this? There is a tradition of special education that has become entrenched. It is hard to break it.

For convenience, the history of special education can be divided roughly into three eras: the first from 1817 to about 1900; the second from about 1900 to 1945 or 1946; the third from the end of World War II to the present.

From the "beginning," in 1817, until shortly after 1900, the residential school was the accepted pattern. This removed the child from the public eye and probably eased the conscience of society since the child was "being taken care of." The residential school was not original to this country, but simply represented a transplant to the United States of the European solution of the times.

Some of the earliest attempts at education of the handicapped are interesting. In 1817, the Reverend Thomas Gallaudet set up a program for the education of deaf children in Connecticut. In 1829, The Massachusetts School for the Blind was established. In 1832, the New York Institute for the

Education of the Blind was opened in New York City. In 1842, New York established at Syracuse a school for retarded children. Michigan, in 1855, set up the Michigan House of Correction for Juvenile Offenders. By 1872 there were twenty-nine state schools for the blind. In short, the belief of the times was that handicapped children should be removed from their normal community settings, grouped together according to the nature of their handicaps, and institutionalized.

As time went on critics pointed out that they, as much as normal children and maybe even more, needed the benefit of close association with their families and parents. A second criticism grew out of the stigma that attaches to the handicapped child when emphasis is placed on the disability rather than on the child and his assets. Schools were commonly referred to as "the deaf school," or the "blind school." A third criticism emerged from the isolated location of most of these schools, which made it difficult for them to provide the quality of teaching staffs desirable and which, in turn, tended to downgrade the quality of the programs.

About 1900 some public schools began to provide day school programs for some kinds of handicapped children. The first day school program for the mentally handicapped was established in Providence, Rhode Island, in 1896, followed by Springfield and Boston in 1897, Chicago in 1898, New York City in 1900, Philadelphia in 1901, and Los Angeles in 1902. By 1911, 220 communities had such programs. Two kinds of schools emerged during this period: those catering to children with only one disability, and those catering to more than one category of disability, with special classes for each category. These schools had some of the disadvantages of the residential school. They were considered more desirable than the residential school because they were less isolated from the main stream of community and family life; but many philosophic and psychological considerations caused the experts to recommend, whenever numbers made it feasible, the formation of special classes within the regular school. The authorities generally agreed with Cruickshank and Johnson:

Segregation intensifies the problem . . . the goal should be to provide contacts with all children as frequently and appropriately as possible.

. . . .

The chief advantage of the special class is that it brings exceptional children into close proximity to normal children, while at the same time providing for those children elements in the educational program which regular class placement cannot effect.[4]

Today, the philosophy of the public schools is much the same. Special classes for the intellectually handicapped are arranged because it is felt these children reach the reading readiness stage much later chronologically than do normal children, achieve at a much slower rate, reach an achievement plateau much earlier, and must have different vocational goals.

The third era started at the close of World War II. There was a tremendous upsurge of interest in the exceptional child, including the gifted as well as the educationally, physically, and emotionally handicapped. This resulted in growth of the number of special educational facilities available.

Some progressive school districts replaced the self-contained special class with a "resource-room" or with more extensive use of qualified intinerant teachers. These were teachers who specialized in education of the visually handicapped, the hearing handicapped, or some other individual handicap, and who moved from school to school working with these children and their regular classroom teachers. Cruickshank and Johnson succinctly sum up the justification for this kind of approach when they say:

4. Cruickshank, William M. and Johnson, G. Orville, *Education of Exceptional Children and Youth.* Prentice-Hall, Englewood Cliffs, N.J., 1958.

In the exceptional child, the concept of individual differences reaches its epitome. There is no such thing as a group of exceptional children if the definition of the group implies basic similarities in the individuals who comprise it.

Merely to group socially maladjusted or emotionally disturbed children together for the purpose of convenience . . . will not solve anything.

To group children with emotional disturbances together creates an artificial situation and places such children under the extreme pressures of the problems of many other emotionally sick children.

The goal of special education is to retain the child in his regular grade placement as frequently as possible. . . .[5]

The trend, then, is away from isolation of the handicapped to a progressively less segregated program. The handicapped child, if he is to be habilitated, must remain with normal children, as a part of the normal school society, to the extent that he can participate profitably.

However, while here and there around the country some isolated efforts are being made to accommodate the needs of the emotionally handicapped child, he is either completely neglected or ignored in most communities.

What is the impact on the community of a policy of exclusion and institutionalization for the emotionally disturbed? By its very nature, the institutional facility is usually geographically, economically, and socially isolated from the community it serves. The specialized facility is rarely attached to only one community, since it is designed to meet a specific need and serves a purpose which a single community cannot support. Thus, it evolves into a unit which does not necessarily reflect the character or values of the very communities it serves. Children removed to these facilities for long term care are exposed to values and attitudes which seldom reflect those with which they must cope when they return. This becomes

5. Ibid.

a built-in stress, frequently unrecognized, and makes the child's return home more difficult.

Equally important is the community's isolation from the problems of the child. Since the solving of the problems related to his special needs is the job of the institution, the community separates itself, ultimately does not wish to deal with them, or fails to develop an adequate procedure for handling any of the intermediate phases. This again acts as a barrier to the smooth transition of the troubled child back into his own milieu.

One of the most distressing of the subtle effects on the community is the elimination of the problem of its population extremes. The result is creeping conformity. All the established units of community function begin to accept, as part of the pattern of problem-solving, the policy of exclusion of the deviate and relegation to the specialized facility. Once this becomes an established pattern, there is a tendency to deal more and more with the median only. Designs of community function become narrower in scope, creating a new extreme which may then be handled again by the process of exclusion or segregation. The community and its organized structure becomes more brittle and vulnerable to any deviation at all. And yet, in most dynamic cultures it is the deviant, the extreme, who often generates the stimulus for adaptation and who may produce the seed for healthy change.

As applied to our educational system, the policy of exclusion now affects well over half a million seriously disturbed grade school children across the nation. Most school districts make no attempt to provide programing for them. In New York State, which has one of the more advanced educational systems in the country, the legislature found it necessary to oblige local boards of education to provide classes for disturbed children, starting in 1966. Rather than consider this progressive legislation, it should be viewed as an attempt to arrest, by the process of internal exclusion, a growing erosion of our established system of compulsory education.

The appearance of the specialized facility within the structure of the educational system also needs examining. This too, has its malignant nature. In New York City, the "600" schools were created to provide special programing for disturbed children—a truly worthwhile effort in its conception. In practice it has become an instrument of internalized exclusion, because it is rarely possible to provide the specialized programs the children need. Not infrequently the "600" schools have become holding units, designed to permit the Board of Education to meet the requirements of the compulsory education law. Other communities are also establishing specialized schools—within their districts if they are large enough, or banded together in county units. This can result only in their eventually falling into the trap of the established patterns, which lead to an acceptance of the principle of segregation and internal exclusion.

This kind of encapsulation ultimately spews forth its poisonous toxins. The educator, sorely pressed as he is, finds exclusion an acceptable solution to many problems. He eventually reaches a point where he consciously believes that his responsibility is the education of the "normal" child, and that the "specialist" must take care of the children with problems. Less consciously, it becomes a solution for budgetary shortages, lack of adequate teaching personnel, and even the emotional inadequacies of some of those responsible for the training of our young. Teaching devices and techniques become standardized to the "normal" and tend to eliminate imagination and individualization.

And what of the children? They are exposed to the monotony of sameness, the boredom of routine, and the mold of conformity. They become indoctrinated in the practice of exclusion as they see members of their peer group excluded, and they accept this kind of segregation as their way of life.

It is conceivable that the growing problem of the school dropout or pushout is related to this. As children have increasing difficulties with the teaching and learning process, they may themselves practice self-exclusion. Their loss of interest in schooling leads them to seek a solution to which they have already been exposed—removal from the system. As they move toward other areas they may be supported and encouraged to leave school by the community and the educator, even though they may be improperly prepared as yet, educationally and vocationally, to take their places in an ever more complex society. A recent major criticism of our educational system was its predominant orientation as a preparatory system for higher education, even though a majority of the students never go on to college. This may be part of the growing brittleness of our educational system as it has become a victim of its own techniques. The major victims, however, remain the large number of children who are excluded from the full benefits of an education designed to prepare them adequately for their future roles in the community.

If these concepts are accepted even in part by society, it does not require much imagination to visualize the effects on every phase of community life. This kind of grouping interferes with the natural process of the community to function as an integrated whole. Special needs are not dealt with and may ultimately, by deliberate exclusion, be swept under the carpet. And so the pattern develops and becomes intensified. Within this construct, if one out of every ten children presently requires special techniques because of intellectual, physical or emotional problems, what will tomorrow bring? No wonder a recent survey produced the astounding suggestion that as high as 70 or 78 per cent of the population surveyed could be considered problems.

It becomes increasingly obvious that the system must be examined. The policy of exclusion and removal of many children to the specialized facility may very well be a principal defect. If it is true that disturbed children can be educated within the community by the public schools, and in the process develop sufficient emotional health to function in the setting structured for normal children; and if the cost need not exceed the amount spent on the normal child (see Appendix), then the public schools have a tremendous obligation to accommodate these children.

What follows is a description of what the public schools of one community are doing. The authors do not suggest that this is the only approach, or the best. It is one method that is succeeding—and it has implications for professionals all across the country.

3 The Elmont Project

UNION Free School District Number 16, Elmont, is in Nassau County, Long Island. It is contiguous to Queens, one of the five boroughs of New York City, and is midway between the north and south shores of Long Island. The greater part of its western boundary is also the dividing line between this school district and Queens. The unincorporated area in the district is a part of the town of Hempstead.

The community is flat, with paved, orderly, treeless streets, few grades, and, like many communities in Nassau County, no large open areas for the use of residents.

Because of its convenient location, it is neither urban nor suburban. It is technically a suburb of New York but it has many urban characteristics. The community itself is not self-supporting and probably never will be, since there is almost

39

no land remaining for industrial development. Because it is almost all homes with neighborhood shopping centers, with no industry other than the Belmont Race Track, most of the residents do not earn their living locally. They commute to New York, or to other Long Island areas with industry. Sperry Gyroscope is a fifteen-minute ride, Grumman and Republic Aircraft are about thirty minutes away by automobile.

There are some, however, who do live and work in Elmont: for example, a small number of professional men. Some business men live and work in Elmont but most shopkeepers commute from New York City, or from other Long Island communities. It is therefore a bedroom community.

There are four community service organizations—Kiwanis, Chamber of Commerce, Lions Club, and Italian Mutual Aid Society—but none of these appear to be a strong, unifying influence. All medical and social agencies are county operated and are located outside of Elmont, with the exception of a public health office.

The school district has mushroomed to its present size only recently. As recently as fifty years ago, a one-room rural schoolhouse adequately served the needs of the district, and the annual school budget totaled less than $1,000. There were several periods of rapid school population growth, each accompanied by increases in school facilities. These occurred in 1924, 1929, and during the post-World War II period, which marked an era of growth that has been equalled by few communities in the entire country. In the thirties there were approximately 2,000 pupils in classes kindergarten through eighth grade; by 1946, there were 3,000 school children in the district; by 1949, the kindergarten to sixth grade enrollment had reached 3,100, plus 535 seventh and eighth grade pupils; by 1960, there were approximately 6,000 pupils in grades kindergarten through six, and another 3,000 in grades seven through nine.

The gross population in Elmont today is close to fifty

thousand. The vast majority of this population is housed in private dwellings that, at today's market price, would be salable in the fifteen to twenty-five thousand dollar price range, with a few running higher and some running somewhat less. Some of the housing is substandard, especially in those areas where garages have been converted into living quarters and which house the population that follows the races.

As might be expected, many Elmont residents are relatively young families, which moved from New York City to an area considered suburban in order to secure its advantages for their children. As school districts go, therefore, it is a relatively poor community. Its ability to pay for education, as determined by the ratio of its real estate value to the number of students to be educated, is low. Give or take a little, there are communities like Elmont all across the country.

The Elmont schools had been committed for a number of years to the principle of identifying and adapting. Eventually the point was reached in 1955 where it became apparent that in order to identify what was operative in some children, the district would have to augment its psychological services with psychiatric consultation. Very quickly thereafter six emotionally disturbed children were identified, in addition to a large number of children in classrooms with varying degrees of emotional overlay inhibiting their school progress. Adaptations within the classrooms and buildings were worked out for the less seriously disturbed, but the six were a problem that could not be handled within the framework of adapted normal programing. These were excluded from school.

As discussions concerning the six went forward hypotheses emerged. It was thought that resources were at hand within the community which, if mobilized, could cope reasonably well with the problems of most of the seriously troubled children. Thus hospital or residential treatment, with their inherent shortcomings, might be avoided. It was further hypothesized that within the community setting such children (including some childhood schizophrenics, children with a diagnosis of chronic brain syndrome, and combinations thereof), while being sustained educationally, could develop emotional and impulse controls. In time, they could function in a normal school setting at their own intellectual, social, emotional, and physical levels. The authors believed that the educational vehicle itself had therapeutic value: if an appropriate educational milieu were structured for the children in which they could experience success, some integration of personality would have to take place. The idea of providing a structure in which these vulnerable children could succeed was basic. Success breeds success, within the hierarchy of human experience, as failure breeds failure.

It is thought that the educative process depends upon, among other things, the child functioning as an integrated whole. The emotionally disturbed child frequently is composed of parts that are not integrated into a functioning whole: if this is true, and if progress is to take place, then the educative process must become the instrument to assist the integrative process.

Educators generally accept responsibility for teaching. What is often not accepted by school people is responsibility for the child as the instrument for learning. Professionals in education accept responsibility for altering teaching as better methods, materials, devices, and techniques are developed and made available—but they generally do not accept the same responsibility for altering the instrument of learning, the child. Not that most children have to be altered in order to profit from the educative process. But some do to insure their readiness or receptivity. Elmont accepted this premise and hypothesized that the instrument of learning, the child, could, in the case of the emotionally disturbed, be altered to enable him to succeed eventually in the normal educational enterprise.

This should be the responsibility of the educator. School-

men generally, and society by legislation, say a child is ready
for school when he is five or six. This is the result of a hundred
years' experience. Actually what they are saying is that children
at that age are in general ready to be taught the predetermined
content, by the agreed-upon common methods, using the normally accepted materials: and that they should, therefore, succeed in the educative process. But this is not always the way it
works. Not all children are at an equal state of readiness at five
or six or any age. The educator has to be ready to try to get the
child, the instrument of learning, ready. It is precisely here
that he becomes a victim of his own devices, for the grade
system is geared to the chronology of the child—and that's
all. Schools must be geared to children's physical, emotional,
social, and intellectual readiness and development. These are
what lead to the breadth and depth and spread of differences
with which teachers have to deal.

Generally, however, teachers are able to deal with only the
intelligence or I.Q. spread, not with the emotional, social, and
physical spread. It's the total of these to which schools must
adapt, permitting the teaching process to become much more
flexible and developing measures of school progress in areas
in addition to the intellectual. Here many professional school
people are blocked because their orientation is to academic
achievement at this or that grade level. We at Elmont hypothesized that if the educational enterprise worked for the
emotional development of these children, it would unlock
academic progress and the children would move forward. Included in this program, then, are not only an intellectual I.Q.,
but emotional, social and physical I.Q.'s. These are used as
measures of a kind, to determine what can reasonably be expected of each child. They form a frame of reference with
which to measure educational progress, on the theory that if a
child grows emotionally or socially it is also educational
growth, and is of an importance at least equal to academic
growth. For the seriously disturbed child this is extremely

important, because until he grows emotionally and socially there is little likelihood that he will grow academically.

A further hypothesis was that a different kind of graded approach, one graded to the child's needs, would be successful. This implied the need for a one-to-one teaching relationship in order to insure the establishment of emotional rapport, which, in turn, could become the instrument or vehicle for the learning process. At the appropriate point in the child's total development the one-to-one would be combined with minimal experience, or with some part-time school experience in the normal school setting. For these children then, the school system had to be flexible enough to get away from standard structure, annual promotions, and the like.

More important, however, was the system's and its staff's willingness to accept the non-professional teacher, the teacher-mom, as a professional. Not a professional educator, but a professional. Teacher-moms, although volunteers, are received as professionals. It was postulated at the start of the Elmont program that they would be treated as such. They are, after all, successful human beings, working under competent educational, psychological, and psychiatric supervision. They are successful and professional because they have been trained by life to be successful child rearers and, by the very nature of this task, teachers. So they are professionals in child-rearing in every sense of the word—maybe sometimes more successful than the technical professionals. True, they were volunteers. Volunteers sometimes are condemned as "do-gooders," but these women were not allowed to become that since by treating them as professionals they immediately achieved status. And in case this were not enough, community recognition for them was promptly built into the structure of the program.

A further hypothesis—more, really, a hope than a hypothesis—was that by attempting to solve the problem of educating the extreme periphery, the seriously disturbed, the problem of educating the normal would also be affected.

A very practical consideration had to be money. Anything done for these children would have to cost little more, if any more, than that spent for normal children, or it would not be possible to accommodate it within the community's educational budget.

To understand the program that emerged it is necessary to know how the school district functions—particularly those services generally included in what educators refer to as "pupil personnel services." Each of the seven schools in the district has its own school physician, employed on a contracted, part-time basis, and its own nurse-attendance teacher, employed full time. There is in addition a head school physician who supervises the work of the school physicians and nurse-teachers, and who makes recommendations for improvements in the district's medical services.

As a result of his exposure to the many psychological problems faced by the school district, the head school physician has himself undertaken a program of study and training at the graduate level. The knowledge and insights gained are passed on to the other school physicians, who, in turn, can facilitate understanding between the school district and the family doctors of the district's children. There is also a supervising nurse-attendance teacher. Assisting on a part-time basis are a psychiatrist (one of the co-authors), an otologist and an ophthalmologist. The nurse-attendance teachers perform a strong social work function through home visits, consultations with parents and related activities, to provide pertinent family information for the staff and, in reverse, to help the home implement school suggestions. The nurse-teachers sometimes work with individual children with emotional problems—by having them help in the nurse's office and, more importantly, by providing the child with a warm relationship with an understanding adult.

The district employs three full-time speech and hearing teachers. They have a direct remedial teaching responsibility for some children with serious defects, a consulting responsibility to classroom teachers as they work with other children with less serious defects, and responsibility for the identification of defects by means of annual speech and hearing tests administered to all children.

The district employs three full-time psychologists as well as the part-time psychiatrist. Their function is to provide diagnostic and appropriate follow-up services for children who are troubled, and, where needed, to assist parents to get follow-up treatment when their own troubles contribute to the maladjustment of their children. (The services of the West Nassau Mental Health Center, as well as other welfare, clinical, and family service agencies, are often utilized to help implement this diagnostic and treatment program.) The team has a preventive responsibility as well. They attend group and individual meetings with principals and teachers: to increase their skills in relating to children; to establish and maintain good mental health climates in classrooms; to develop skill in early identification of children in need of help; and to pool resources when providing help.

Two full-time visiting teachers work with the permanently and temporarily homebound children of elementary school age. They instruct the homebound child in basic subject areas that parallel the programs in his age and grade level at school.

Four part-time supplementary teachers work with emotionally disturbed children in the schools on a one-to-one or small group basis. They provide tutoring and remedial instruction as do the visiting teachers, but in the regular school buildings, outside the regular self-contained classrooms. These services are scheduled on an individual basis as they are needed, by joint decision of the psychologist, classroom teacher, and school principal.

Three full-time helping teachers, who specialize in reading, work to improve instruction in basic subject areas. They act as consultants to classroom teachers, and in a direct teaching capacity with individual children or small groups of children who require remedial tutoring. In many cases these include children whose academic deficits are possibly the direct result of an emotional overlay.

The district employs special subject teachers in the areas of art education, music education, physical education, and library services. In addition to their responsibilities to the general school population, these special subject teachers are an important adjunct to the district's program of special adaptations for the child with emotional problems who cannot tolerate a full day in the self-contained classroom. His program is, therefore, structured to include extra periods of art, music, physical education, library work. The subject matter, as well as the close relationship with a special teacher, seems to help. Decisions for such special programing are made after inter-disciplinary staff conferences, which include representatives from all the special services, classroom teachers, and any others whose involvement with the child can shed light on diagnosis or recommendations.

The philosophy of grouping in Elmont is to recognize its necessity, but to accomplish it in such a way that the child is not lost in the group. Instead, the group itself becomes an instrument, in a limited sense, to help the child's intellectual and emotional growth. This is accomplished by evaluating facets of personality that need to be considered, the child's adjustment to teachers and classmates of varying personalities, the strengths and weaknesses of the child's academic achievement, and the teaching and personality strengths of individual teachers. Thus, to the extent it is feasible, each youngster is matched to the teacher who probably can contribute most to his development.

The objective, then, is "harmonious" grouping, that is, heterogeneous ability grouping, but narrowing the range of differences a teacher has to deal with and matching teacher and group to child. When the principal and teachers have completed the preliminary work in connection with grouping, the school psychologist reviews the placement of each child in the building to insure the proper implementation of the district's grouping policy. Retentions and accelerations, too, are reviewed individually by the school psychologist.

Despite these facilities the school district has, as do most, a number of children whose degree of disturbance is serious enough to preclude progress in normal classrooms, and disturbing enough to inhibit the progress of the class. To provide some organized educational facility for these atypical children, the school district embarked on the Project for Exceptional Children.

These youngsters are the seriously emotionally disturbed. Generally speaking they are intelligent, although variability in I.Q. measurement is expected, as is their performance—from day to day, and often even from hour to hour. Their behavior is often unpredictable. They are hyperactive, aggressive, distractible, impulsive, compulsive, irritable. They have difficulty in abstract thinking. They are anxiety-ridden, emotionally immature, perseverative. Usually they are school failures. Not all of these children show all these characteristics, but all show some. It is this that makes it unwise to work with them in a normal classroom.

Elmont is convinced, for reasons already discussed, that special classes, another group approach, are not the answer to this problem. From a characterization of these children as well as from related literature it appeared that the kind of program needed would have to be custom-made for each child: to reduce distractibility to a minimum, and to establish a one-to-one relationship between pupil and teacher. Group activities would need to be included, and on-going psychiatric and psychological guidance would need to be provided for the children and the staff. No school district, including Elmont, which is relatively unfavored economically, can afford to provide a teacher for each pupil and the space to minimize distractions to the degree needed by these children.

Recognizing these factors, and faced with the problem of an ever present group of these seriously disturbed children, the district set about to create, for the 1959–60 school year, a specialized program within the established educational framework of the community. The general objective was to provide each child with an individual education and training program based on his identifiable needs.

This is a critical issue and, in a sense, does battle with some of the concepts generally accepted in public education. Education is based, of necessity, on the mass production principle. However, some children will not tolerate this approach. To the degree possible, therefore, there has to be built into the system the concept of adapting the system to the child, and not the child to the system. It is interesting to observe that, traditionally, special classes are developed to accommodate to the special educational needs of exceptional children. These classes become special units, but they are, again, only a modification of the mass approach. There has to be built into the system the concept of total adaptability, if the public school's responsibility for the education of all the children of all the people is to be discharged. The challenge to school administrators and boards of education, then, becomes one of developing systems with the capacity to adapt.

The problem of moving public education toward adaptation takes priority over all other problems confronting the schools. The Elmont school district underwent a long period of frustration, struggling to contain in regular classes children who could not tolerate a large group situation. This period took its toll of teachers, the education of the other children in the group, and the handicapped children themselves. The frustration was twofold—inability to identify the problems of some children, and inability to accommodate even when the identification could be made. But as the district developed the

resources and sophistication to identify it also had to develop
the ingenuity to adapt. At the present time it operates within
the concept of total adaptation of the system to the needs of
individual children, and not the reverse. There is still much to
be done in this regard, but the system is now immunized so
that never again will it be able to revert to a position of mass
rigidity. The ability and willingness to adapt is the immuniza-
tion.

The new approach involved building into the system a
program of early identification. Everyone, the board of education, the administration, teachers, pupil personnel staff, school
secretaries, and the community, had to be sensitized. The
special project for seriously disturbed children, which is the
concern of this book, became a point of contagion and helped
stimulate adaptations to the needs of children all along the
line. Now the system can adapt forever, because increasingly
its people are able to accommodate with minimal anxiety.

But there was a risk, too. As the skills of identification were
honed and the tools of adaptation developed, the broader the
problem became. Perspicacity in identifying leads to more
problems, and more complex ones, as staff awareness is sharp-
ened. It is only a short step, from successful adaptation to the
gross problems of children, to the need to adapt to the individual needs of all children. It took the Elmont district four
years to infect the system to the point that its professionals
graduated from saying, "We've identified, what are you [ad-
ministration] going to do about it." Now they say, "We've
identified, what can we do about it." Now the professional
disciplines seem able to get together and work out adaptations
around a child, and, while they sometimes are unable to alter
their own behavior, they are able to work out a program built
around the individual.

This implies a multi-educational approach requiring the
educator to break down the educational progress into parts,
for example, the "look-say" method in reading, or the phonetic

approach. However, some children need a "holistic" approach. They need to be glued together before much educational progress can be made. It therefore becomes the job of the educator to try to hold them together while educating them. It is precisely this that some of the adaptations in the school district, as well as the special project for troubled children, attempt to do.

Implicit, too, is the concept of rationing the educational effort. The educator has only so much to give. Educational administrators are always making decisions about where, on a priority of need basis and to the neglect of no child, the effort should be put. It is at this point that the educator is maneuvered into a position where he must mobilize community resources. It is doubtful that any school system in the foreseeable future will include, in itself, all the resources needed to cope with the problems of identification and adaptation.

To produce a program to accommodate to these needs became, then, an educational administrative problem. The task became one of finding several available classrooms and teachers for the six original children on a one-to-one basis, as well as a sponsoring organization to assist with the financial support. The ultimate goal of the educational program would be individualized training through optimum relationships, and final reintroduction of the child to the regular classroom without ever totally separating the child from the family or community. By providing the necessary specialized program within the context of a one-to-one relationship and preventing the child's exclusion from the community, it was felt that the educational program itself could become therapeutic to the child. (A basic premise of this approach is that proper education and training can be a therapeutic process.) Done within the established framework of the family and community, the disruptive effects of separation anxiety could be eliminated. If successful, perhaps these children could the sooner be returned to regular classrooms, able to function in a group and not

handicapped by educational deficits serious enough to constitute a barrier to their adjustment.

In casting about for a possible solution it seemed that all
the resources needed were at hand in the community, but
either unorganized or under jurisdictions unconnected to the
Board of Education. Since space was not available in the
schools (there were 6,000 children in buildings with a rated
capacity of 4,800) space would have to be provided, and free
of charge. As in almost all communities, there were areas not
normally used during school hours: church halls and base-
ments, Fire Department meeting halls, the American Legion
dugout. A neighbor, the Elmont Jewish Center, was just completing a building with ten classrooms, an arts and crafts
room, kitchen, playground, and even an outdoor swimming
pool. This seemed ideal. Permission was asked and received
to use six classrooms mornings, and any of the other facilities
the program needed. The Rabbi was sympathetic enough to
imply that if the children caused some damage, his board
would understand. The Board of Education agreed to supply
transportation for the children, a teacher supervisor, the psychological and psychiatric consultant services, and books and
supplies normally a part of the district's equipment.

The Elmont Kiwanis Club agreed to provide some financial support. For instance, the club paid the premiums to
insure the Jewish Center and the staff from suits should a
youngster be injured. It also provided about six hundred dol-
lars for special equipment, such as two-sided easels and flannel
boards for each child, electric answer boards, large locked steel
cabinets in which to store and secure gear and equipment, and
milk and cookies for daily snack time.

The most difficult problem, however, was how to procure
a teaching staff in numbers sufficient to provide a one-to-one
relationship. Furthermore, the kind of people needed—warm,
empathic, mature, emotionally stable, dedicated—are difficult
enough to find even when salaries are available.

There were in Elmont, as in most communities, women of this kind who had done a good job with their own children, and who were in a position to contribute some of their time to community activities. From among such women came the "teacher-mom." No broadcast appeal was made, so there was no need to refuse the help of people not suited to the work. Through personal contact, a number of mothers were invited to contribute two mornings each week to working with a child —the work to be done with supervision from the professional staff. They were interviewed by the administrator and the psychologists. Every effort was made to discourage them by painting a dark picture of what they were about to get into. These interviews provided a good opportunity for the professionals to get some insights into the volunteer herself. It was felt that if two mothers were teamed and assigned to a particular child two mornings a week, this would come close to resolving the problem of the one-to-one relationship. There was no trouble in securing the original twelve teacher-moms to start with the six children (now expanded to thirty-eight, working with eleven children).

The teams were thoroughly briefed by the professional staff concerning the child with whom they would be working. They were given educational materials appropriate for the child and a sketchy introduction to the methodology of teaching, and the enterprise was under way. An early elementary school teacher was detailed to the project to assist the teacher-moms as needed, and to supervise and coordinate such details as supply and transportation. The school district's administrator, the psychologists, the head school physician, and the psychiatric consultant worked closely with the teacher-moms as they began to feel their way toward helping these children.

Specifically, what do teacher-moms do? A routine day might go as follows: The teacher-mom meets her project child as he gets off the station wagon, escorts him to his assigned room and helps him stow his gear and clothing. She then takes him to the "good-morning" room, where the professional teacher-in-charge is waiting to conduct the opening group exercises. These consist of the salute to the flag and a short reading and discussion period. The reading and discussion evolves from what the teacher-in-charge has written on the blackboard, or from "show and tell." She tries to include sentences at the reading level of each of the children which, when put together, make a paragraph about the day's weather, or a holiday, or an event, or something with which the children are familiar. Discussion is encouraged. The opening exercises may last a very few minutes or as long as fifteen, contingent upon the manageability of the group that day.

While this is going forward the teacher-mom has secured the books, games, and equipment she plans to use that morning, and is in her assigned room ready to receive her child when he returns from the opening exercises. She sits next to, and close to, the child, and the day's work begins.

She may begin with reading, usually using the reading series and supplementary materials available to the professional teachers of the district. She is encouraged to follow the teacher's manual more closely than a professional teacher, because the manuals are well developed guides and provide comprehensive directions on how to teach the series with which she is working. From reading she moves to other subject areas, such as arithmetic, spelling, language skills, social studies, science. These activities, interspersed at her discretion with games, or talk, or a walk, or listening to records, go forward until 10:30 A.M., at which time there is a snack break. She takes her child to a large room with a long table and benches. One of the children and his teacher-mom have laid out the cookies and milk beforehand—which is done on a rotating basis. All the children as a group sit down and have their snacks under the supervision of the professional teacher-in-charge.

While the children are having their snacks, the teacher-moms usually assemble in the kitchen for coffee and cookies. Here there is much discussion of the project children, although sometimes it is more social conversation than professional. The snack-time and coffee break takes fifteen or twenty minutes, at the end of which the teacher-mom returns to her room to continue work with her child, following the plan for the day as agreed upon with the teacher-in-charge. If other group activities are scheduled they usually occur during the time between the end of snacks and the end of the morning. At 11:45 the teacher-mom begins to get her child ready to go home. At this point she completes her log of what transpired with the child that day, and leaves it with the teacher-in-charge so that it is available for her teammate teacher-mom.

In the course of the morning she has probably been visited by the teacher-in-charge, who provides on the spot direction and suggestions for furthering the child's educational program.

This is a reasonably normal morning. There are some mornings that are not normal, however, because these children vary in their behavior and responses from day to day, hour to hour, and sometimes minute to minute. What the teacher-mom brings to the child is her own emotional climate—that of an affectionate, understanding mother. Her empathy with the emotional needs of the child may result in her altering his academic program, even to the point where it is discontinued. When she senses tension building in the child she is free to lead him away from the academic learning experience by playing a game, taking him on her lap, going for a walk. This leads to a relationship learning experience, which frequently obviates academic or emotional failure for the child. She may even decide to remove the child completely from the structure by taking him to the firehouse, or the post office, or just out on the playground.

She must be perceptive enough not to respond to provocation by the child. Here she may lean heavily on the teacher-in-charge or the psychologist, even to the point of having the other professionals take over completely for a short period of time. Sometimes the teacher-moms have teamed up to handle an acting-out child. In short, the teacher-moms are constantly interfering with the expected, disturbed patterns of these children. This they are in a position to do promptly by virtue of the one-to-one relationship.

She must use her judgment and imagination at times to help the child overcome his academic learning difficulties. The result has been the utilization of some highly unorthodox teaching methods and materials. With the assistance of the teacher-in-charge and the psychologist, because the teacher-mom recognized that the child retained little or nothing of what had been taught over the past few weeks, learning programs have been modified even to the point where a child has been stopped and started all over again. Incentives such as cookies, candy, stamps or coins for a collection have been used. One teacher-mom found that by allowing her project child, a girl, to fix her (the teacher-mom's) hair she could return the child to concentration for another period of time on the learning task. A teacher-mom began to recognize in Donald, who will be described later, a need to be fed as he was taught, for, as he put it, it was "brain-food." Perhaps for him it was, since by ingesting food and learning simultaneously he was providing himself with two ingredients essential for survival. Another teacher-mom, working with Edward, found that allowing him to stand up and move about helped him concentrate. She even made use of his preoccupation with clocks, not by removing the clock but by keeping one close enough so that his preoccupation was channelized, thereby permitting another part of him to concentrate on reading or arithmetic.

A group activity of about twenty minutes' duration was provided toward the middle of the morning, which included arts and crafts, music education, physical education, or story time. Other group experiences included the daily snack-break of milk and cookies, and the children's riding together in the school district's station-wagon bus to and from school. Each child's birthday was celebrated by a simple party during snack time. The teacher-moms supervised these group activities on a rotating assignment basis, usually two or three to an activity. Increasing use is being made of the playground facilities for free play and organized games, and seems to be working reasonably well.

The program has been in operation now for five school years. Six children aged six to eight comprised the original group. Up to eleven children have been accommodated at any one time. To date, a total of thirty-one children have been included in the project at one time or another. Of these, twenty-one have been successfully returned to regular classrooms, one has been hospitalized, and one moved out of the district and is functioning in a regular class part-time.

How well the Elmont program and approach supports our basic hypotheses is perhaps best delineated by the case histories—the stories, to follow, of some of our children.

4 The Disturbed Child: Case Histories

Introduction

MANY young children enter our school systems poorly organized and ill-equipped to take the stresses of group living and formal instruction. They can be readily recognized by their inability to adapt to the regular classroom situation. These children are identified by regressive or disruptive behavior, failure to function successfully with their peers, and disorganized learning ability which serves as a frustration to both child and teacher. When such children are studied in order to identify the roots of their difficulties a wide range of causative factors can usually be found. It is rare that a single disturbance will disrupt a child's total pattern of functioning. More likely, several disturbances within and around him have a causative relationship to his disorganization and inability to learn. When these disturbances are severe, even superior in-

59

telligence cannot compensate for his disorganization, and the result of the attempt to educate is non-learning or meaningless learning. This process can be seen clearly in the schizophrenic child who, by definition, reflects a total disorganization in all areas of adaptive behavior and functioning.

These children are true human enigmas. They have all the parts but they are not a unified whole. As they attempt to function, their own internal disorganization interferes with their natural capacities and the normal demands of growing and learning. Attempts at adjusting to regular social living cause them to malfunction. They use various devices and defenses, which further isolate them from their peers. Their patterns of functioning serve them poorly in all their life experiences. Some of these patterns are so deviant they can be called psychotic mechanisms, and these are so bizarre that the child is judged as being beyond all the limits of the normal. Without respect to their innate capacities, such children, as soon as they are identified, are frequently excluded from school, isolated, and directed toward institutional care.

Another group, though equally disorganized in basic personality, seem to be able to structure their functioning in acceptable ways, but ways which do not serve them well in their attempt to grow. This neurotic organization of personality frequently keeps the child on such an emotionally immature level that all his attempts at living are constantly disrupted. But because his manner of functioning resembles our own he is acceptable, although a constant frustration. These pseudoneurotic schizophrenic children represent a large block of unidentified learning problems that constantly frustrate educators.

Another group within this broad category are those who give up their capacities rather than continue to experience the stress and anxiety of their inability to adapt. These pseudodefective individuals have locked within them the potential for performance. But because of their vulnerability and lack of integration every task of living and learning becomes a painful experience. They can take just so much pain. The process of growth, with its constantly expanding spiral of demand for performance and more complex function, becomes a torture rack on which these children exhaust themselves early in life. In some instances even the loving, tender care of well-meaning parents is unable to relieve the pain of this internal disorganization, and the child removes himself into another world—a world of isolation and loneliness, identified as autism. But at least it is a world free of the pain of disorganized perception and function.

When the process is not quite so severe, unwillingness to look and learn becomes the instrument of withdrawal. If this goes on long enough, then to all intents and purposes the child functions defectively. This pattern may become so entrenched that he cannot be identified as separate from those children who actually have a fixed deficit.

There is yet another group that fit the category of seriously troubled youngsters. These are the children who, as they attempt to cope with living, experience pain and stress and become motivated to attack and destroy what they view as the source of their pain and stress. Unfortunately they are rarely aware of the internal disorganization which makes them so vulnerable. Exposed to the demands of their growth and the social structure to which they must adapt, they first ineptly strike out at things around them. As they grow their ineptness is replaced by organized antisocial behavior, leading to refusal to learn and delinquency.

They refuse to learn because they would be confronted, then, with their own internal disorganization: should this occur they would experience the pain of their own vulnerability. Thus a vicious cycle is established which seldom can be disrupted, because anti-social behavior and non-learning have become the principal instruments by which they have learned to survive. This psychopathic organization of personality not only becomes a disruptive process to the individual child, it also eventually becomes a threat to his peers, the educational system which must teach him, and, finally, the society which must contain him. It is easy to see how, in the natural course of events, such children ultimately breed their own exclusion and isolation and finally must be institutionalized: not for their own good, but for the protection of others.

This constellation of troubled children represents a great challenge to the educator. Most of them come into the school system with their vulnerability well established and their patterns of coping with life already formed. All too often this process goes unidentified. The educational system unwittingly intensifies the child's vulnerability and stress, and accelerates the movement toward the already existing psychopathic mechanisms within him.

The educator may thus become an unknowing partner to the child's abnormality. The child's withdrawal is complicated by the educator's use of exclusion. His immaturity is enriched by the teacher's frustration. His learning difficulties are compounded by a lack of communication. His anti-social behavior is rewarded by social ostracism.

If anything is to be done to help these children, certainly they must be identified early. But early identification itself will serve no purpose unless an adequate system can be developed to help them function with less stress, less anxiety, and less failure. It must be remembered that the pain, frustration, and failure stem from their own internal disorganization. This is why teachers must have more training in the basic principles of child psychology, and educators must join forces with the psychologist and psychiatrist.

Most young children have these problems to some degree. Therefore the educator must develop a system adaptable to the needs of children. The education enterprise must have, first, a range and breadth capable of identifying vulnerability and stress, and second, the innate capacity to compensate for vulnerability and minimize stress. If this can be done for the type of children described, it can certainly be accomplished with even greater impact on the healthy development of all children.

Human experience is the best laboratory for the evolution and development of ideas, methods, and practices. What follows is a description of some of the specific experiences in the Elmont project. They demonstrate the vulnerability, the stresses, and the methodology which emerged in solving some of the problems, and which finally led to a theory and practice of adaptation to the needs of children within an educational setting.

The Psychotic Child

First is the child whose bizarre behavior has always isolated him, destroyed his chances for social and intellectual success, and made a mockery of standard teaching devices because of his internal distortions in ideation and motivation.

This child, whom we shall call Steve, was identified almost immediately, upon entering kindergarten, as a troubled youngster. He was aggressive, destructive, deliberately distracting, didn't share, demanded attention, was moody, had temper tantrums, and when upset made animal noises instead of talking. He was unable to relate or respond to any of the usual, or even extraordinary, overtures of the teacher. His behavior frequently was unrelated to the group activity or the instructions given. He was hyperactive, clumsy, poorly coordinated, and functioned as if he were composed of parts that had never quite coalesced. By the end of the first grade it became obvious that he could not be kept in classroom. Initial psychological testing included only the SRA (Science Research Associates) Group Test of Intelligence, which revealed an I.Q. of 132; it had been impossible to complete the administration of the Stanford-Binet because of the child's uncooperativeness. Steve was referred to the local mental health clinic for psychiatric evaluation. The diagnosis was schizophrenic reaction of child-hood.

Information obtained from a number of sources, including direct contact with the parents, revealed a long history of disturbed behavior within the home prior to starting school. However, because of various circumstances, his behavior was accepted by his parents. Some of the information disclosed that Steve had always been hyperactive and difficult to manage. He ate compulsively, with many food idiosyncrasies. His hyperactivity extended into much rhythmical body rocking, which started quite early in the first year and persisted through the time he was first involved with school. He was preoccupied with fantasy play, which became so consuming that his mother was unable to distract him. She herself offered the opinion that Steve became so absorbed in his fantasies that he made them his reality. Prior to his enrollment in school he had isolated himself from his peers and been rejected by them. He had a sister three years his junior, whom he frequently abused and physically attacked without apparent provocation. As a young child he had many fears and had difficulty falling asleep. His sleep was interrupted by frequent nightmares. He alternated from total detachment and absorption in his fantasy to a clinging, dependent relationship with his parents.

Not only was this disturbance a basic part of Steve, but extensive contact with his parents revealed considerable disturbance within the family. The parents had severe problems of their own and with each other. They too alternated from total detachment to spasmodic, intense involvement with each other and Steve. Their involvement, however, was not always a constructive one, since it seemed to have intense sadomaso-chistic components. As a result the family climate was a stormy one, constantly fluctuating and filled with intense periods of unhealthy emotional crises, alternating with periods of isolation, separation and unrelatedness. This disharmony had always existed, and continued in spite of extensive professional efforts to mitigate it for the sake of the child. The parents frequently talked of divorce and even went so far as to take initial actions leading to legal separation. This occurred several times over the period of the school's contact with Steve. There have been periods of planned separation, stemming primarily from the family difficulties rather than from the natural course of events.

Within this family climate, Steve's own problems could only be nurtured and encouraged. Both parents were highly motivated to help their child, but could not accept either professional recommendations or alternate courses of programing for their youngster. He therefore continued to be exposed to their inconsistent efforts in the parental role. Thus a sad but vicious cycle of interaction between child and family was established, which served only to perpetuate the already well-entrenched distortions within the youngster. Certainly this set of personality disturbances by their very nature could lead him only into a world of isolation. It placed the educator in a position where his sole alternative, for the sake of the other children in the classroom and the mental health of the teacher, would be to send Steve into the world of exclusion.

It was with such a child and life situation—and others— that the special project of the Elmont school district was begun in 1959.

At this time Steve was an obese child of seven, with a chubby but handsome face and light brown hair. His cheeks were often red and there was a rough, course quality to his skin, which was even more noticeable in the winter. His facial expressions were unpredictable. They ran the gamut from beaming to scowling, from happiness to anger, from pleading to rage. At the time Steve entered the project he was reading only on a first grade level, despite his obvious high intelligence. He had unusual arithmetic skills and in this area performed on a third grade level. But in other areas he functioned somewhere within the level of the first grade.

He was assigned to teacher-moms who were given sketchy outlines of his basic problems, with emphasis being placed upon the child's own inconsistencies and those to which he had been exposed. Their primary instructions were geared to the need for consistency in spite of failure, and appropriate communication at all times in spite of Steve's apparent lack of ability to follow instruction. They were to seek a constant relationship in spite of rejection, disruption, and his attempts to achieve isolation, and above all to offer, in spite of all attempts on Steve's part to destroy the relationship, consistent emotional warmth. Within this structure the teacher-mom was permitted the widest latitude and selection of devices that, in her judgment under the supervision of the teacher-in-charge and the psychologist, might appeal to Steve.

The general objective of this kind of approach was the introduction of a consistent, meaningful relationship as an instrument for the development of appropriate communication. By conscious design, it was meant to introduce and maintain Steve in a learning situation which would bend, but not break, to his disruptive efforts and tremendous fluctuations in mood and purpose. At the same time it was planned to utilize this youngster's rich capacity for fantasy, directly channelizing and blending some of his own specialized interests into the area of learning. This procedure, which could be implemented only by an individual approach, was designed to anchor his fantasy onto the realities of a learning situation involving real knowledge of the world about him. Finally, in a purposeful manner, his impulse problems and difficulty with controls were, wherever possible, deliberately channelized into repetitive tasks that are readily found in the learning situation. Here again individualization was required, as well as the imagination of the teacher-mom, the supervising teacher, and the psychologist.

It was felt, from both a psychological and psychiatric point of view, that if any of these objectives could be sustained they might have a therapeutic benefit. The interrelationship between the teacher-mom and the child was thought of as a highly individualized teaching-learning situation rather than a therapeutic one: however, with a child like Steve, a successful teaching-learning relationship must become therapeutic. The role of the school psychologist and the consulting psychiatrist remained at all times one of continuing identification, advice, and support for the teacher-in-charge and the teacher-moms. The instrument of therapy was education through the teacher-mom and the teacher-in-charge.

It is interesting to note the many devices used in relationship and teaching, as well as the youngster's progress within the project itself. There were periods of very good to very poor adjustment. Some of his academic interests and needs determined the program and the time schedule offered him. Some of the fluctuations at home caused episodic regressions, with poor general functioning, loss of control, and a consequent continuing need to modify the overall program. After a year in the project Steve was tried with a part-time, gradual transition to a regular classroom a day a week for part of the afternoon. But severe intra-family crisis caused a regression and led to the termination of his participation in the class.

In some of his periods of regression Steve demonstrated a compulsive need to be first in everything, particularly on line, in the group situations structured for the children of the project. This generally made for additional problems in peer relationships and in his development of such social concepts as sharing, taking turns, or fairness. This intense emotional need to be first certainly complicated his social relationships, and reflected his constant confusion, so characteristic of the schizophrenic process, in values and symbol formation.

Within the teaching-learning relationship, however, his need was successfully used to introduce a sequential sense to the learning process itself. As his periods of regressive behavior subsided. Steve could use some of these acquired patterns for more successful functioning. It took well over three years for a gradual improvement to develop in this area, but develop it did, so that by June, 1962, he often could accept a lesser position within the group without being upset. It was at this point that Steve and his parents again accepted referral to the mental health clinic and became productively involved in a psychotherapeutic program.

Although many of Steve's behavior problems persisted they gradually modified; everyone concerned felt there was distinct improvement. To coincide with this, Steve showed the greatest progress in the area of relating to others and in accepting and demonstrating affection, particularly with adults. His hypersensitivity and fear persisted; he could be threatened easily and intimidated by children much younger or smaller than he. His developing capacity to use his intellectual skills then became a method by which he attempted to relate to others, or he would use it as an instrument of aggressive behavior.

Steve frequently tended to perseverate thoughts and actions. He often had difficulty transferring his lines of thinking from one area to another. This tendency was utilized to lengthen his attention span around areas of learning that needed strengthening. At various times this perseverative nature would interfere with the introduction of new learning situations, and certainly new social interactions. However, since everyone concerned with Steve was constantly alert to this problem, errors were not perpetuated for too long a period of time.

After several years within the project, Steve became able to acknowledge and verbalize about his inter-personal difficulties. This enabled the teacher-moms to discuss these problems and worries with him, and in this way they were able to help him somewhat with his management and control. It is interesting that as he became more successful Steve gave up one of his fantasies, that of being "Superboy," and again became more amenable to the educative process.

A point was reached finally where, because of impressive educational progress, Steve found it to his advantage to retreat into learning rather than into fantasy. As a result he made amazing progress educationally during the five years of his stay in the Elmont project. As part of a research program during 1962–63, he was tested, both educationally and psychologically, at the beginning and the end of the school year. The results speak for themselves; they should be judged in terms of the initial levels of his functioning, plus the rough estimates of his capacities when he entered the project.

In September, 1962, a California Reading Test (grades 7–9) was administered. Steve scored as follows:

Reading Vocabulary	7.2	
Reading Comprehension	9.8	
Reading Total		8.0

A California Arithmetic Test (grades 7–9) was also administered. The scores were:

Arithmetic Reasoning	11.0	
Arithmetic Fundamentals	10.5	
Arithmetic Total		10.8

It should be noted it was felt the ceiling on this test was not sufficiently high for this child.

On the language section of the California Achievement Test (Form E) Steve scored:

Mechanics of English	6.5	
Spelling	7.9	
Language Total		7.2

The psychological tests administered included:

Wechsler Intelligence Scale for Children:
    Verbal Scale IQ   144
    Performance Scale IQ   131
    Full Scale IQ   141
Bender-Gestalt Visual Motor Test
House-Tree-Person
Thematic Apperception Test
Rorschach

Analysis of these test results showed Steve to be functioning at borderline genius level of intelligence. His projective material still demonstrated the schizophrenic process and the many accompanying neurotic components. Within the content of the tests, tremendous control problems were evidenced along with a generalized picture of pan-anxiety, with emphasis in the area of fear of disintegration in a hostile world. There was evidence of distortion in body-image. His human figures were seen as giants or monster-like and threatening. A struggle to maintain roots or boundaries to the point of constriction was seen in some areas, together with the opposite extreme of uncontrolled expansiveness. Many of his responses indicated an active fantasy of a highly explosive quality. There was also an overall immaturity on an emotional and performance level despite his high intellectual capacity.

Repeat educational and psychological evaluations were performed in May, 1963, at the termination of the research year. Designed to identify the progress of the children and some of the operational mechanisms, they were highly revealing of the changes taking place within this youngster. A California Achievement Test (junior high level) was administered with the following results, and compared with the September, 1962 scores:

Reading Vocabulary	12	(a gain of more than five years)
Reading Comprehension	10.4	(a gain of six months)
Reading Total	11	(a gain of more than three years)
Arithmetic Reasoning	12	(a gain of more than one year)
Arithmetic Fundamentals	11	(a gain of one year)
Arithmetic Total	12	(a gain of about two years)
Mechanics of English	7.8	(a gain of one year, three months)
Spelling	8.2	(a gain of three months)
Language Total	8.0	(a gain of eight months)
Battery Grade Placement	10	(a gain of about two years)

The most marked area of academic change was seen in reading. The gap between Steve's reading and arithmetic scores was narrowed to about a year, the greatest growth being in reading vocabulary (more than five years). This caused his academic profile to appear more uniform and would facilitate his placement in a regular school setting, if and when he appeared ready for this on a social and emotional level.

Since Steve's basic problems never really were his academic skills, the most critical areas appeared in personality integration. Psychological test material revealed some of these changes. On the Wechsler Intelligence Scale for Children, he achieved a verbal scale I.Q. of 147; a performance scale I.Q. of 136; and a full scale I.Q. of 146.

The test analysis showed that Steve continued to function at the borderline genius level of intelligence. Although he was still preoccupied with fantasy and somewhat expansive, this was much less grandiose than in the fall during the initial testing. The schizophrenic process and the developing neurotic components continued to be readily identifiable in all of the projective material. His anxiety, compulsivity, perseveration, psychosexual problems, and confusion in his own identification, all persisted. Impulsivity and anxiety were still very dominant. He appeared to function in a more organized fashion, however, with less retreat into fantasy. Although it was obvious that Steve's problems were still very severe, it was felt that significant progress of a quantitative nature definitely appeared in all areas.

Some of these quantitative changes were observable directly in his behavior within the project. Periods of regression, although still present, were not so long and sustained. When he became argumentative, restless, and uncooperative, he could more easily be persuaded, through his dependent relationship with his teacher-mom and the supervising teacher, to conform to the demands upon him. The unevenness in his academic achievements narrowed, and with this came a greater willingness to accept new and unfamiliar areas of learning. Eventually some of this began to spill over into his social functioning; he did make attempts at interrelationships with his peers with a greater willingness to bend to the demands of the situation.

It is interesting to look at the teaching methods and materials that were used with this youngster. Steve always preferred to set his own schedule and pacing. He had difficulty following a superimposed time schedule. He was able to sit and work for long periods of time, up to two hours at a stretch, but once the work pattern was broken by snack or group activities it was almost impossible to get him back to work. Therefore, within the structure of the specialized program, Steve was always scheduled for a late snack. His academic programing was run together as much as possible, using the device of saving for last the subject he was best at and from which he got the most enjoyment. His pattern of learning consisted of reading, writing, language arts, social studies, mathematics, and science.

It is important to note that in terms of teaching methods and materials, conventional instruction, as outlined in teachers' manuals, has always worked well with this child. There has been heavy emphasis on independent and silent activities, and frequent tests to evaluate achievement. Steve was never able really to take instruction within a group. He worked best independently, and more recently in the one-to-one teaching situation, as he sought relationship with his teacher-moms. He has enjoyed setting his own limits, time-wise as well as work-wise. He has learned best from books as opposed to people. He has enjoyed measuring himself against the standardized norms. Steve always disliked writing, although he enjoyed reading and responding orally. His resistance to writing was circumvented within the individualized programing.

The main educational materials used with Steve during the 1962–63 year included:

Dictionaries: intermediate and teacher's desk
Language arts books: grades 5 and 6
Arithmetic books: grades 7 and 8
Social studies books: grades 5 and 6 (many publishers' offerings)
Library books in science, space, travel
Heath Health Series: grades 5 and 6
Noble and Noble, *Fourth Grade Handwriting Workbook*
Readers Digest Skill Builders
Current Events
Weekly Reader
Boys' Life
Cuisenaire arithmetic rods

As one reviews the problems presented by this youngster—the investment of material and human resources, and the progress he made, there is little question of the value of the effort. Because of his own and his family's problems, their severity and persistence, it is safe to assume that during the five years of educational programing he could not have been contained in any existing classroom setting involving group instruction. Yet, during this period of time, not only has Steve been helped to preserve and use his intellectual skills, he also has been helped into a much more vital area of sustained human relationship. Today he stands motivated to seek relationship with the society with which he must live. His progress, as of this writing, is permitting a gradual transition into the group learning situation to which he never previously adjusted. In order to preserve his academic progress and the potential for a gifted and productive intellectual life, he must continue to be helped in the area of social living. His self-chosen isolation is gradually becoming more painful to him than his reality. His need for acceptance and communication is gradually replacing his magical thinking and omnipotence. There is little question that, through the instrument of the one-to-one relationship, this child's intellectual and concomitant educational skills have been preserved. He has been led slowly and sometimes painfully into the area of human relationships as an acceptable way of life.

To judge the true progress of this youngster, consider the possible alternatives to the Elmont project. Exclusion from every group learning experience would have been his inexorable fate. Under such circumstances, in contemporary society, unless the child comes from an extremely wealthy family this means an educational death—whether he is maintained at home or in a residential facility. One need not range far from personal experience to see many people bred within the community whose educational progress was halted prematurely because there was no school program adapted to their needs.

It might be argued that this child would have benefited from residential placement early in life, since he would have been removed from the disturbing influence of his family. The argument does not stand up. The most intense effort, over the past two decades, to mobilize community resources for the establishment of residential facilities, has resulted only in a few spread across the country—barely enough to care for a few thousand children. These facilities have become so expensive to operate that few communities are willing to maintain them. Certainly the weight of professional experience and scientific knowledge would suggest that almost as many problems are created by placing a child within a residential setting as are solved by such a program. Who among us would take a child away from a family that wants it and is willing to clothe and feed it and give it love—even if this love may be complicated by the emotional problems of the parents. In Steve's case, his parents received the help that was recommended and participated in programs designed to modify their way of life to the best of their ability. They even requested appropriate placement for him when they recognized their inability to preserve a home for him because of their intense dislike for each other.

It is appropriate to report that, at their request, it is now planned to move Steve into a residential treatment setting—

not a mental institution—in an attempt to preserve the gains already witnessed and to try to establish further gains. This action is particularly significant in the light of their rejection of this kind of approach in previous years. They themselves have witnessed the improvement in their child through the efforts of others; they remain sufficiently devoted to him to desire these gains to continue; and they recognize that they are unable to make the necessary changes themselves that could help Steve to continue to progress.

What seems to be of equal importance to his progress was Steve's retention within his community and family during the important formative years of his life. The early developmental years are critical for human relationship. Steve had always demonstrated the greatest problem in this area. In spite of difficulties his retention was in the basic arena of human experience, the family and the community. The primary battle for Steve to become a functioning member of the human race, rather than a species of his own fantasy, seems to have been won. Although he is still quite problemed, it is the consensus of those who have been most closely involved with this youngster that he has learned finally to accept human relationship as a *modus vivendi*, painful as it may be. Prolonged institutional care is a notorious bandit of normal human and social values. It steals and destroys human experience necessary for survival in our complicated social structure.

In this vital role as guardian of the intellectual and social growth of the young child, the educator fulfills his responsibility as he identifies and adapts to the child's needs. Certainly, in the extreme situation of Steve, a child incapable of group instruction for most of his formative years, a great contribution has been made by tiding him over and helping him to reach a point where it is now possible for him to grow and develop. His situation reflects an extreme. But so much can be learned, by solving the problems of the extreme, that have application to the middle. Through dedicated application to Steve's problems many effective devices were developed that permitted more successful and rapid changes in some of the other children. In his own particular manner, Steve made his contribution to the overall educational effort.

The Neurotic Child

In the course of the development of personality in some children, exposure to subtle stresses serves to impede normal integration. When these stresses occur at critical times and in vital areas, the child's personality may be so distorted that malfunction appears in every aspect of his behavior. He may be so motivated to defend himself against these stresses that he has extensive difficulties in functioning in areas meaningful to his social and intellectual progress. Most often these defenses are mobilized in direct response to the stresses, and the resulting behavior is frequently unrelated to many of the child's life situations. If this process is extensive enough, it may end in total disorganization of personality, deviant behavior, and serious problems of adjustment.

Such is the story of Donald, who is a handsome, slim, dark-haired youngster. He is always seductive, charming, affable, agile, and somewhat elusive. He is of average height and weight for his chronological age and his physical development is normal. He first came to the attention of the school psychological services in kindergarten. His adjustment to kindergarten was marked by difficulties in peer relationship, hyperactivity, and a general inability to conform to the simplest of classroom routines. By 1960, at the age of eight, his maintenance within the normal school setting had become a problem. He was transferred to the special project because of extensive disturbance within him and in his immediate neighborhood—although it was seldom possible to identify him positively as the cause of the latter.

Donald's family situation was marked by open parental incompatibility, discord, and other individual emotional disturbances. His parents were separated once but resumed their chaotic family life. Unfortunately, Donald and his younger brother, who is eleven months his junior, were most often the recipients of their parents' hostility, which otherwise would have been directed at each other. The mother tended to punish both boys very severely. She resorted to strenuous beatings or deprivations in varying degrees. Both boys had difficulty adjusting to kindergarten. Since they entered school in 1957, however, the younger brother has shown consistent improvement while Donald has deteriorated. The family constellation of these children was further complicated by the presence of paternal grandparents and other relatives in the immediate physical vicinity, subjecting the boys to many inconsistencies and differences in attitudes.

As an unfortunate result of the school district's policies regarding birthdates at that time, Donald and his brother entered school simultaneously. They were placed, at the parents' request, in the same class. The initial adjustments of both children were poor. It was later discovered that Donald and his brother had had minimal contact with other children outside their home, since they were rarely permitted to go out for free play. No stimulating experiences were encouraged, and the normal curiosity of childhood was discouraged and suppressed by the attitude of the parents. The mother also vacillated in setting boundaries of behavior for her children, and fluctuated from constant reinforcement of limits and complete rigidity to a laissez-faire attitude, leaving the boys to manage by themselves.

By the end of the kindergarten year referral of Donald to the school psychologist was necessary. At that time, testing and clinical observations revealed inconsistent thought processes, inadequate and inappropriate concept formation, fragmentation, and perseverative tendencies. There were some distortions in visual-motor perceptual organization. He needed immediate gratification of impulse. His imagination was prolific. Day dreaming was a constant problem, with most of his satisfaction of needs taking place on the fantasy level. The psychological and psychiatric diagnostic impression at that time was that of schizophrenic reaction of childhood with neurotic components.

Referral to the local mental health clinic was initiated. While Donald remained in treatment at the clinic, little progress was made by their professional staff toward incorporating the parents into a meaningful counseling program on any sustained basis. At the conclusion of a two-year treatment program for Donald, marginally supported by his parents, minimal improvement was reported. The family was followed sporadically for the next year or so, and finally treatment was terminated by the clinic.

As of January, 1960, Donald's maintenance within the normal school setting became impossible. His behavior was becoming more difficult to predict or manage. He was seen as being in the process of building, in an attempt to survive, an impenetrable wall about himself. He was becoming more inaccessible, defiant to authority and generally negative. He was anxious and confused and frequently experienced guilt which tended to immobilize him. His emotionally impoverished early home experience provided him with little opportunity or base for the development of positive relationships. At the time of his transfer to the Elmont special project he achieved an I.Q. of 83 on the Kuhlman-Anderson Test C, which is a group testing device. At the same time he was functioning in all academic areas on a second grade level, which was compatible with his chronological age of eight.

After a stay of several months in the special project he was returned to the regular school setting, partly because of the hostile attitude of the home, partly because of his overall improvement. He was not able to maintain himself, however, and had to be readmitted to the special project within a few months. The following school year another attempt was made, with specific support provided on emotional and academic levels by having the teacher-moms accompany him into the regular class setting. Yet, even with this specialized program, it became increasingly difficult for him. He again returned to the special project for the next school year. Successful transition to the regular classroom setting was finally accomplished during the 1963–64 period, and this transition seems to be a complete one.

It was obvious, from the very beginning of the school's contact with Donald, that his primary problems rested in his emotional development rather than his intellectual performance. His behavior, all too frequently, reflected what was known of his personal difficulties. Thus, the primary objective in transferring this youngster into the special project was to give him direct, intimate, one-to-one relationship with adults, within the structure of a learning situation. It was hoped that by consistent exposure to warm, flexible, yet reasonably well-structured relationships, the disruptive practices which constantly plagued this child could be interrupted. At the same time it was hoped that his educational progress might be preserved, since his disruptive behavior in the normal group classroom required his exclusion for the sake of the other thirty children. His exclusion was required also to relieve the pressure on the teacher. Even though he was moved back and forth between the project and the regular classroom, all the well-established relationships were constantly preserved for the child. It was the specific objective to sustain all meaningful relationships that might be of help to him.

Donald's scheduling was, of necessity, always flexible. Because his academic ability was poorest early in the morning and improved gradually as the day progressed, most of his meaningful learning experiences were given to him later in the school day. Because the group situation always led to a breakdown in his controls and extreme hyperactivity, he was maintained in a one-to-one relationship with the teacher-moms most of the time.

The pacing and timing of Donald's actual program were usually as follows: reading, drawing, arithmetic, arts and crafts, language arts, with about fifteen minutes for each activity. Donald was calmed by art work, which is why this form of activity followed and preceded each of his academic subjects. Spelling seemed to tire him excessively and was deliberately left for the end of the morning's learning session. This type of programing worked successfully only on his good days; on bad days, no amount of flexibility or rigidity or any other device seemed to be effective.

To date, no pedagogy has worked too successfully with this youngster. Varied approaches have been attempted on both a group and one-to-one basis, using various conventional and sometimes unconventional supplementary materials, all to little avail. The least unsuccessful of the approaches involved the use of music or art, which were Donald's special interests. He made a picture book for use in social studies. He was given special instruction on the trumpet and the drums. He continued to resist academic programing.

He was very sensitive to the grade level markings of any material he worked with, and he regularly compared them with the materials his younger brother used. It was found that Donald would do arithmetic more willingly if it was done on the blackboard where mistakes could be erased. To encourage him in reading, he and the teacher-mom alternated in reading paragraphs from the book.

Handwriting lessons were integrated with spelling. Donald worked best standing up, and he was permitted to do so. Constant physical activity appeared to help ease his tensions. He responded poorly to pressure, and so the academic program was structured permissively. He was frequently permitted to select his own activity, and if it was done satisfactorily he was rewarded with permission to select the activity following. Music and art also were used as rewards and incentives, as were food and candy, which this child called "brain food."

It appeared possible to teach Donald by repetition and rote, but the learning was not applied and was not deemed meaningful. It was obvious that Donald's psychological problems interfered with his learning.

The materials used in Donald's education during the 1962–63 year included:

Models of dinosaurs, cars, planes
McKee and Harrison, *Let's Write*
Weekly Readers (editions 3 and 4)
Readers Digest Skill Builders (grade 2)
Eye and Ear Fun
Nicky
Silver-Burdett, grade 3 speller
Scott, Foresman, grade 3 readers and workbooks
Ginn & Co. grade 3 readers and workbooks
Ginn & Co. grade 5 reader, *Trails to Treasure*
Ginn & Co. grade 5 reader workbook, *Trails to Treasure*
Follet, *Indians, Settlers and Pioneers*
Highlights magazine, grade 4 social studies
Arithmetic flash cards, crayons, drawing paper, charcoal
Silver-Burdett, *Making Sure of Arithmetic* (grade 3)
Silver-Burdett, *Making Sure of Arithmetic Workbook*
Supplementary arithmetic materials for Silver-Burdett
Lippincott *Phonics Books* (A–G)
Health Science Book, grade 4
Snare drums, tape recorder, trumpet

During one year that he was at the project Donald was part of a research program devoted to the identification of changes and progress in the children. As a result, specific educational and psychological testing was available at different times. In January, 1961, his grade level scores on the California Achievement Test (E) were as follows:

Reading Vocabulary	2.5	
Reading Comprehension	3.9	
Reading Total		2.9
Arithmetic Reasoning	3.3	
Arithmetic Fundamentals	4.7	
Arithmetic Total		4.1
Mechanics of English	3.5	
Spelling	3.7	
Language Total		3.6

In September, 1962, on the California Achievement Test (U.P.), Donald scored as follows:

Reading Vocabulary	4.2	
Reading Comprehension	3.9	
Reading Total		4.0
Arithmetic Reasoning	4.0	
Arithmetic Fundamentals	3.6	
Arithmetic Total		3.5
Mechanics of English	4.0	
Spelling	3.5	
Language Total		3.8
Battery Grade Placement		3.8

It was noted that Donald appeared to think mechanically and without reasoning logically. This frequently resulted in a non-sequitur type response to many seemingly simple situations. His thinking was quite disorganized; he appeared very flighty, going from one trend of thought to another without logical or apparent connection between the two. He would be unable to complete a verbalized thought, and he would even forget what he originally set out to do or communicate. He told "tall tales" and appeared to believe them himself. He was unable to follow directions or suggestions and he was distracted by the mere presence of another child in his room. When Donald had to do anything by himself he would go off into fantasy almost instantly. Even with close supervision, he would try to digress from his task to talk of unrelated things.

Psychological testing administered in September, 1962, revealed a full scale I.Q. of 88 on the Wechsler Intelligence Scale for Children, with a verbal score of 82 and a performance score of 96. The score was considered minimal in light of Donald's inter- and intra-test variability, plus the obvious emotional blocking. The projective test material revealed him as presenting most of the problems already described. There was also a severe problem in the area of sexual identity and role, with some attempts at masculine identification in spite of many frustrations and fears, seemingly stemming from female stimulation, specifically on the part of his mother. There was a distinct concern with the need for strength on both an internal and external level. This could constantly be seen in his attempts to imitate masculine behavior, such as fighting or pushing. Many defensive suspicious attitudes were displayed, masking paranoid tendencies. His inaccessibility at any given moment reflected his consciously felt need to maintain his integrity in the face of impending disaster. His apparent need for instinctual satisfaction had grown as a result of the lack of need-satisfaction in infancy and early childhood.

Donald's impulsivity and strivings to maintain control in the face of possible breakdown presented the most serious problem. His conflicts with his environment, and his unsatisfactory inter-personal relationships with his family, continued to force him to obtain satisfaction on a fantasy level. This, in turn, seemed to perpetuate his feeling of detachment, and of the need for caution and constriction, in an attempt to survive in what he considered a hostile setting.

During his overall stay in the project it was possible to witness the phenomena mentioned and to observe changes— which ultimately became highly significant in his emotional and social development, but not in his educational achievement. He often displayed a great deal of resistance and generalized anxiety. In addition he was resentful, manipulative, overly defiant, hostile, aggressive, and negatively tenacious. Demanding behavior, perfectionism, and compulsivity masked his underlying fearfulness. He demonstrated extreme mood swings, was often depressed, and was extremely sensitive to the nuance of another individual's behavior or approach toward him. He was sometimes verbally or physically abusive or withdrawn, and, seemingly, completely out of contact with his reality. At other times he was friendly, ingratiating, and humorous. He used fatigue and other somatic complaints to avoid work. His overt attitudes made it extremely difficult for anyone to establish, let alone maintain, a meaningful relationship with him. He even attempted, with every technique at his disposal, to mitigate the potential success of any program undertaken in this area on his behalf.

After a long period there was a glimmer of meaningful change in Donald. This was reflected in his ability to sustain a given learning situation, a more appropriate state of awareness, and less volatile, hostile, demanding, and negative behavior. A proportionate decrease occurred in his generalized anxiety and fearfulness.

In the initial stages, Donald saw himself as a bad, stupid, disliked, and very unsuccessful person. He was dissatisfied with his life, his accomplishments, and the picture he presented to the world.

He finally began to demonstrate some changes in his own attitudes and self-image. He no longer consistently condemned himself. By May, 1963, Donald indicated that he saw himself as sometimes good and sometimes bad, bright but stupid at times, nice looking, never fearful, both liked and disliked by his parents, fairly successful and content with being a boy, and satisfied in general. His projective material did not completely support this self-image, although a major change along positive lines was clearly and dramatically indicated. There was the beginning of appropriate male identification. He demonstrated less fragmentation, and a greater sense of intra-personal balance, better controls, and the establishment of various functional modalities for handling a variety of stimuli.

His hyperactivity, always a major problem, began to change, with Donald demonstrating an ability to control his impulses, establish boundaries for himself, and accept limits. Accompanying this was an increase in his attention span. There were less frequent instances of aggression on another child, less irrational and unpredictable behavior, and a slight improvement in his level of agitation. Even his speech patterns were not so erratic or easily affected. His low frustration level continued to be a problem and frequently resulted in ending an academic situation. But for the first time, Donald demonstrated a willingness to wait for the gratification of his needs. He also tended to offer reasons for his inability to perform, sometimes even projecting the fault onto another. A total breakdown of controls no longer seemed imminent, and a calmer façade prevailed.

Donald had always relied heavily on his ability to suppress or consciously control situations, without any real awareness of his ongoing resistance toward many situations and people. Here, too, significant changes seemed to take place over a period of time. Fantasy, which originally assumed such importance in Donald's life as his means of escaping from a hostile world, now appeared to be taking a more appropriate position in regard to his total functioning.

His greatest problem was in the area of relationship with others. On the occasions when he was unable to relate to his teacher-moms his affect became vague; he was detached and completely indifferent to their attempts to break through his reinforced wall of inaccessibility and isolation. He was sometimes belligerent or very hostile to them. At other times he was able to relate, seemingly needing to air his feelings and his family problems. Ultimately, he was able to verbalize many of his feelings to them.

Disciplinary action was usually met by a response of indifference or negativism. He was distrustful of the purposes and motivations of others. His reaction to any expression of acceptance and affection was a product of his mood of the moment, and was often unpredictable. Physical contact, smiles, demonstrative actions, or verbal praise thus elicited a variety of responses, and frequently one of indifference. He strongly demonstrated an inability to relate appropriately to adults, a suspiciousness regarding their unpredictability and a generalized distrust of their motivations. This made it very difficult, and, at times, impossible to reach Donald. Although he needed limits in order to function and was covertly anxious to please his teacher-moms, his façade denied both and an attitude of indifference prevailed. Many times during the year his teacher-moms questioned the efficacy of the program for Donald, as well as the value of their own contribution. Few discernible changes occurred in this area throughout the year, although major improvements began to appear toward the end of his stay in the project.

A key factor in his changing attitude appeared to be Donald's ability to sustain a relationship with the music teacher. He made remarkable progress with the drums in a relatively short time, and his singular success seemed to be transferred to overall levels of functioning. Most important was his increased tendency to respond in either positive or negative fashion, as contrasted with his former indifference. He now appeared to be able to interact with people and his capacity for relating appeared strengthened. A major transition began to take place in his emotional attitude. The same subtle change began to appear in his peer relationships, and gradually Donald began to react more appropriately, both to individuals and groups. Interestingly, his cooperation with family and project personnel seemed inversely related. When his mother reported an improvement at home project personnel noted deterioration, and vice versa. But without question,

Donald began to develop more appropriate social attitudes as some of his own internal disorganization abated.

Donald was reevaluated educationally and psychologically in May, 1963. A California Achievement Test (Form E) was administered with the following results, and compared with the September, 1962, scores:

Reading Vocabulary	3.8	(a gain of 4 months)
Reading Comprehension	4.7	(a gain of 8 months)
Reading Total	4.3	(a gain of 3 months)
Arithmetic Reasoning	5.2	(a gain of 1 year, 2 months)
Arithmetic Fundamentals	4.0	(a gain of 4 months)
Arithmetic Total	4.6	(a gain of 9 months)
Mechanics of English	5.7	(a gain of 1 year, 7 months)
Spelling	4.0	(a gain of 5 months)
Language Total	4.6	(a gain of 8 months)
Battery Grade Placement	4.5	(a gain of 7 months)

Although on the surface there appeared to be little improvement in Donald's behavior he did manage to progress academically in all areas: he appears to have been learning imperceptibly, and in spite of himself.

On the Wechsler Intelligence Scale for Children Donald achieved a full scale I.Q. of 101, with a verbal score of 91 and a performance score of 111. These results clearly indicate an improvement in his overall functioning ability. The scores, particularly on the performance scale, came closer to his previously estimated potential. The most positive changes appeared in the projective test material, which revealed a definite stabilization of ego strength. He indicated increased ability to cope with his environment, which now appeared less threatening although still a source of conflict. The establishment of more appropriate modalities for obtaining need satisfaction was suggested. Problems in the area of his psychosexual identity and role persisted, but Donald appeared to be in the process of developing appropriate male identification. On the surface he continued to display many defensive suspicious attitudes. But the need for such attitudes no longer seemed predicated on the overwhelming nature of his internal fantasy and preoccupation with threatening material. His paranoid tendencies had markedly decreased and his inaccessibility was now an outgrowth of emerging concern with things around him, rather than those within him. Donald's impenetrable wall seemed designed to provide him with opportunities to develop greater ego strength. This method, although very difficult for the teacher-moms to understand, was successful for him, and his own collapse of control no longer seemed imminent. There was still evidence that he continued to satisfy his needs in fantasy, but there were also indications of an externalization of interest in this area. As noted in the projective material, his imagination and fantasy life remained prolific, but the content was now much less anxiety-producing and more appropriately channelized. His Thematic Apperception Test responses demonstrated constriction and a definite attempt to handle the stimulus presented in a concrete, reality-based manner. He introduced an emotional affect that was now far more appropriate, and there was no suggestion of bizarre thinking. He was better able to cope with boundaries and limits, while exhibiting a relatively calm outward affect. Inconsistent thought processes continued to be a problem, although his ability to sustain a given thought and to concentrate had increased. There was less fragmentation of thought noted, and fewer perseverative tendencies.

Donald has been successfully transferred back into his appropriate grade and is functioning with a minimal amount of difficulty in a normal classroom setting. Certainly one cannot point to tremendous educational gains as the outgrowth of special programing. However, from the various observations and test results, it is quite apparent that many of his internal problems have been successfully assaulted and modified by the specialized approach. The critical issue involved rests clearly on the question as to whether the educator should assume any responsibility for the internal emotional life of a child. Since growth and development take place on an integrated level involving not only the child's intellectual, but also his emotional, social and physical life, it would seem that the question posed is an artificial one. Donald and the history of his changes certainly confirm this. His academic progress left much to be desired; yet, as a result of specific efforts geared toward solving his critical problem of human relationship, his intellectual functioning improved. As we have continued to observe him, his social integration has demonstrated equal growth. Here is an example of a school program effectively helping a child to approach his potential, which is the primary goal of all education.

The Pseudo-Retardate Child

Among the most unfortunate of disturbed children is that group which seemingly give up or lose their birthright to live in the world—those who for complex reasons, fail or refuse to acquire the means for communication adequate to the demands for normal growth. When looked at carefully they seem to have all the necessary parts, but they are either unable or unwilling to expend the energy required to help these parts coalesce into a meaningful, operational whole. The result is a self-destructive effectiveness which robs them of the basic equipment necessary for survival in an increasingly complex life. These pseudo-retardates are a constant frustration to both parent and professional. Their functioning *parts* seduce the adults concerned with them. Their non-functioning *whole* consistently frustrates. The result is an ambivalence that contributes further to breakdown of meaningful communication.

The saddest part of the story of these children is their ultimate fate. Their façade of defective functioning dooms them to a life of dependency, and most of them, since they are unable to take the ordinary stresses of living and must be protected constantly from the impact of man's aggression, end up in long term institutional placement. In their own way, these children represent one of the greatest challenges of child-rearing. If they can be given even limited facilities for appropriate communication and helped to achieve minimal integration of function, they often can become self-sufficient.

More specifically, these children remain total educational disabilities as long as they are permitted to preserve their disrupted system of communication and language formation, and retarded functioning. There are thousands of such children in the country, and the challenge they present to the educator is that of helping a child gain the *equipment* for the learning process rather than simple exposure to learning itself. At present the prevalent attitude is that the educator's responsibility is for the learning process alone, and that he should be absolved from involvement with the necessary equipment. But these children are an enigma to the educator. He cannot understand them. He ultimately must reject them—and so he does, since almost all of these children, as quickly as they are identified, are excluded from the school systems and constitute the core of the "attic" children. Efforts made in Elmont in behalf of these children have exposed the system to one of the basic contradictions that plague the educational enterprise. Unless there are heart and conscience to direct educators' energies to the equipment as well as the process, many will be deprived of maximal development. If the problem of educating and training these children can be resolved all will benefit: for a heart will have been structured into the system.

One of the outstanding successes of the Elmont approach was with such a child. The success itself is not a complete one and the final chapter has not been written; but her story illustrates what an appropriate program can do to develop the equipment for learning and then the learning itself.

Dora is a slim, blond, hazel-eyed child with a pasty complexion. She is generally neat and clean, but her clothes usually appear to be mismatched or ill-fitting "hand-me-downs." Her hair is chopped off at about ear level and is even all around. She wears glasses and at times seems to squint. Her general demeanor is that of a quiet, withdrawn, anxious, tense child.

Dora is the younger of two children. A brother, three years her senior, has always attended school in the same district with no major difficulties reported to date. The family is a troubled one, constantly marked by a full gamut of marital conflicts. The father is a chronic alcoholic who is sporadically employed. The socio-economic level of the family is marginal. Both parents were European-born and emigrated to the United States just before World War II. Their history has always been poor. The mother seems to be the dominant figure in the household, despite a passive façade. Because of their financial instability she works from time to time as a domestic.

Dora had been recognized by her parents as having problems, their particular concern being her lack of speech. Prior to initial contact with the school district and for years thereafter, Dora's mother sought the advice of nearly every major psychiatric, psychological, educational, and speech facility in the New York City area, but with no sustained effort to maintain the contact once she was offered a course of action. Upon entering the school system at the age of five, Dora had not yet acquired recognizable speech. Her reported diagnoses included aphasia, early infantile autism, organic brain damage, schizophrenic reaction of childhood, and primary behavior disorder. Regardless of diagnosis, however, the various agencies concerned concurred on a poor prognostic picture.

When first seen upon her enrollment in kindergarten in September, 1957, this youngster was severely withdrawn and incapable of functioning with her peer group. Inter-personal relationships were virtually non-existent. She was totally dependent upon her mother, and her only other meaningful relationship was with a cat. According to the history offered by the mother, the child's development was normal except in the area of speech. She walked at thirteen to fourteen months, was toilet trained by one-and-one-half to two years, and began to feed herself by age three. She had always been hyperactive and clumsy but reasonably easy to manage. Most significantly, her mother was able to say she had no trouble communicating with her child, since, as she frequently said, "I know what she wants to say without her having to say it."

As a result of her inability to adjust to the group and the lack of development of recognizable speech, a second year in kindergarten was recommended for Dora. There was some slight improvement during this school year. She was able to function on the periphery of the group, although direct interaction with another child or group of children was rarely seen. At various intervals during both years, speech programs were attempted but discontinued because of Dora's lack of readiness.

At the conclusion of her second year in kindergarten, Dora's minimal progress in all areas, including lack of recognizable speech, inappropriate responses, and severe possessive tendencies, suggested that placement in the special project was desirable. By this time the symbiotic quality of the mother-child relationship also had been identified, and the need to alter its destructive nature was recognized as the core problem if a meaningful teaching-learning process was to be developed.

Dora entered the special project in October, 1959, with no usable speech and functioning on a pre-school level in all areas. Objectives were simple but heroic. Dora was to be taught the need for communication, encouraged in its use, and rewarded by the warmth and pleasure contained in human relationship. The teacher-moms were specifically instructed as to these objectives. All else was secondary.

The primary objective was deliberately described in terms of breaching Dora's dependence on non-verbal communication. At the same time it was recognized that this child had serious problems within the integrative areas of functioning of her central nervous system. She had obvious visual-motor perceptual problems which might interfere with the acquisition of some of the basic instruments of learning. Therefore, on a secondary level, the teacher-moms were indoctrinated into methodology involving simultaneous exposure to visual, auditory, and kinesthetic cues. The idea was for the teaching process to become both the integrative force and the instrument for acquisition of basic learning technique. Her program was weighted with equal responsibility between the teacher-moms and the supervising teacher, so that her emotional and educational needs were met simultaneously and could further serve as a pathway to learning.

She remained in the special project for a year and a half. During this time, the development of the relationship between the child and her teacher-moms was designed to interfere with the symbiotic parent-child process. Conversation, although largely one-sided, was encouraged. There was almost constant use of concrete material of visual, tactile, and auditory qualities. In spite of the lack of language an approach to reading readiness was initiated, as well as some simple arithmetic work and group activity. Dora's response to the reading work was immediate, positive, and sustained, whereas other activities required a much longer and gradual development before they were accepted and attempted. During the course of the year and a half, her educational program was expanded to include the usual first and then second grade curriculum in reading and arithmetic. Simultaneously a great deal of improvement was observed in her speech, which seemed, to a large extent, to be an outgrowth of her reading progress.

By the end of her first year in the Elmont project Dora's response to her teacher-moms had become spontaneous and enthusiastic. Her attempts at verbal communication increased and became constant. She relied less and less on gesticulation and pantomime. This presented somewhat of a problem, since her speech frequently lacked clarity. However, her frustration level increased with the passage of time, and she would repeat something upon request without becoming visibly upset or withdrawing. She desperately sought approval, which she was given at every possible opportunity. By the end of the first year it was agreed that she had developed enough speech for the addition of a structured speech program.

In January, 1960, the Arthur Point Scale of Performance, Test II, 1946 revision, was administered. An I.Q. score of 81 was obtained and thought to be minimal in light of the concentration of items requiring motor coordination, which was one of her principal problem areas. This was the first time she had been successfully tested and was the first record of intellectual capacity approaching normal. That same month, a Revised Stanford-Binet Scale, Form L, was administered. At that time she had a chronological age of 7.1, with a mental age of 5 years and 10 months, giving a full scale I.Q. of 82. Here again this was estimated to be minimal because of the extensive problems in language.

In the midyear of the 1960–61 school session it was agreed that Dora should be reintroduced to the regular school situation on a part-time basis, looking toward a full-time enrollment. This was accomplished with few adjustment difficulties, and the full-time program followed shortly thereafter. In May, 1961, the Wechsler Intelligence Scale for Children was administered. She achieved a full scale I.Q. of 80, with a verbal score of 86, and a performance score of 78. Despite her general function in the border area of dull-normal intelligence she was able to maintain her grade level relative to her chronological age, and she functioned in the middle reading group in her second grade class. By the end of the school year her achievement indicated normal promotion to third grade.

Dora's progress in language arts and social studies was maintained at grade level. Speech improvement was sporadic and continued to show difficulties. She mispronounced certain letters, such as "l" and "r," and when excited there was definite regression. In arithmetic she had little success. She continued to have difficulty with basic concepts beyond simple addition and subtraction.

In September, 1962, on the California Achievement Test (UP), she achieved the following results:

Reading Vocabulary	3.6	
Reading Comprehension	3.8	
Reading Total		3.7
Arithmetic Reasoning	3.5	
Arithmetic Fundamentals	3.5	
Arithmetic Total		3.5
Mechanics of English	4.0	
Spelling	3.6	
Language Total		3.8
Battery Grade Placement		3.65

Dora was now in a regular fourth grade class in school, with teacher-mom help two hours each week. She had become an active member of the group and demonstrated her ability to sustain learning within the group setting. She continued to show some deficits in arithmetic concepts. In this subject as well as speech improvement teacher-mom help was needed. Her severe speech problem continued in evidence, but Dora had learned to use language as the basic instrument of communication. She had learned to read orally. She was speaking volubly, although unclearly, and responded in a positive manner to praise and encouragement. She continued to withdraw when criticized and persisted in being particularly sensitive to facial communication, such as smiles and frowns.

In May, 1963, she achieved a full scale I.Q. of 79 on the Wechsler Intelligence Scale for Children, with a verbal score of 74, and a performance score of 89. By this time the results appeared to be reasonably accurate and reflected Dora's total functioning. She had difficulty in handling manipulative materials, yet her overall operation in the performance area was better than in the verbal area. It was difficult to evaluate adequately her capacities, as her strengths or weaknesses varied from test to test. In the projective material she continued to demonstrate a weak reality boundary, but seemed to attempt to hold on to it. She was in the process of repressing disturbing fantasies, and there were indications of marginal controls. Anxiety, feelings of weakness and ineptness, were woven into the fabric of her responses and probably account for the drop in verbal score. However, she continued to demonstrate social facility with both adults and peers, which seemed to be improving all the time. There was less questioning and fearfulness of strangers, as she attempted to converse and relate to other children. There were signs of emerging sexual awareness, ambivalent feeling toward her parents, and an ever present frustration in her attempts at functioning.

In light of the total experience with Dora it was the opinion of the professional staff that sustained support on a one-to-one basis was still needed, and she was given this through the use of remedial speech and the continued partial use of the teacher-mom.

Dora's progress, when viewed from her point of departure, can be judged truly phenomenal. However, the final story is yet to be written. During the past year she continued to show progress within the teaching-learning situation. There was increasing evidence, however, of a reactive pattern, seemingly related to her awareness of the turmoil within her own home. From reports which she herself was now capable of giving, there was evidence of some deterioration in the family. Dora's perception of this made her extremely anxious and seemed to stimulate her, from time to time, into a kind of active withdrawal into fantasy. It was almost as if the original impairment of perception, which permitted her to subsist within her family, were now confirmed as a defensive device. Now that her perception and communication had been welded into a usable instrument she showed signs of reacting to the pain this instrument caused her. But to her own credit let it be said that she seemed to be working hard to preserve her integrity, and seemed also to be painfully winning the battle.

From an educational point of view, there is little question that the program offered this child had been meaningful and successful beyond all hopes. There is also ample indication that Dora has, within her own substance, the wherewithal to use both her natural and acquired equipment in the ongoing struggle for successful living. It remains to be seen whether or not she will ultimately survive the rigors and stresses and complexities of human experience. But there is little doubt in the minds of the professionals that those adults who helped have fulfilled their delegated responsibility to teach her the ingredients of awareness, communication, and the joys and pains of living and learning.

The Sociopathic Child

Probably the most frustrating and demanding child with whom the educator must deal is the youngster who wishes to attack and destroy the human relations around him—and consequently his own educational and social experiences. Since he does this in an unknowing, constantly repetitive manner, his perception of the pain stimulated in himself and others is dulled. He becomes oblivious to the process within himself. He begins to live in a strange fortress from which he sallies forth to attack indiscriminately innocent bystanders. He subsists within an isolated bastion, constantly building thicker walls to defend himself from attacks to come and never realizing that these ever growing defenses serve only to dull his perceptions of the world around him.

The ever growing opaqueness of his defense serves only to

destroy his learning capacity as a growing human being. The teaching relationship becomes a constant frustration to both the child and the teacher. Ultimately the child justifies his attack on the relationships in the educational situation as a means to destroy the system, which constantly engenders in him a sense of frustration and tension. His behavior takes on easily recognizable anti-social qualities. He becomes disruptive to the teaching process and aggressive toward his peers within it. His anti-social behavior subsequently acquires semi-delinquent and finally outright delinquent qualities.

When this process is unaltered it produces the sociopathic and psychopathic personalities so disruptive of society. These children cannot be taught normally because the teaching process is alien to their intrinsic motivations; social values cannot be communicated because they go against their grain.

Such children represent educational dilemmas. They provoke and challenge. Frequently the educator is seduced by such aggressive provocation, and then must face the failure of his teaching approach. Sooner or later he must do something about his own sense of frustration and, if unaware of the true source of the interaction, may end up with the same kind of aggressive and destructive attitude toward the child. The end of such an interaction can only be exclusion, for with it the source of the frustration, the child himself, is eliminated.

When this takes place, a new dimension is added to these children's world. They feel justified in the construction of their fortress. They intensify their search for new weapons to strengthen their citadel. They begin to seek allies in their war on the society that drives them into isolation, and, with exclusion, they frequently join the delinquent group. The group gives them an identity; it protects them from the pain of the process of exclusion and isolation.

Some of these patterns were present in Edward, an attractive, well built, light-haired, dark-eyed youngster of ten when the school district decided to move him into the special project. He had very early presented an adjustment problem and given little evidence of the academic progress justified by his normal mental ability. He had received individual instruction in the regular classroom whenever possible, and many special provisions had been made in an attempt to permit successful learning. When he entered the special project he was a non-reader and was untestable in language usage. In arithmetic, he was functioning on a second grade level.

In April, 1961, prior to his movement into the special project and as a result of several serious incidents involving assaults on other children, Edward was suspended from school and placed on home teaching. He had been constantly disruptive in the classroom. He had been involved in petty thievery. There had been several minor episodes of fire-setting with which he may have been connected. He had difficulty in relating to peers. He tended to participate on the periphery of the group, or seemed to be an active negative force in its midst, aimed at disrupting whatever was in progress. He was distrustful and suspicious of adults and needed to test them time and again.

Psychiatric evaluation at the time of his exclusion from the regular classroom identified speech articulation problems, a peculiar constellation of concrete thinking associated with denial and repression, poor self-concepts and primitive body-image formation, and a fantasy view of his world as empty. There was evidence of a depressive reaction with an apparent intent on preserving what little reality he had, for whatever it was worth. In spite of all his difficulties, and of his awareness of his suspension from school, there was little or no evidence of anxiety or of any kind of guilt associated with his misbehavior.

Some of his family experiences closely correlated to the identifiable features within his personality. He was the youngest of five children and the fourth boy following the only girl. He was brought up by all members of the family with many interchanges in role, since both parents were usually employed and displayed little interest in the welfare of their children. Through long contact the school had learned that this family stimulated little motivation for scholastic success. This attitude, and the accompanying lack of concern about his behavior, had led the school authorities to choose suspension from the regular classroom as a means of highlighting to the family the school's concern over Edward's behavior. The parents were totally unreceptive to the suggestion that they seek guidance for their youngster, and managed to communicate their attitude that it was the school's responsibility to solve the problem of handling him.

At the time of his admission to the special project, all personnel were carefully briefed as to the objectives. Educational progress was considered secondary to the social goals. It was deemed essential to establish and maintain relationships, even at the sacrifice of educational progress. He was to be tutored in human emotions. Social values were to be offered as one of the prime objectives of the teaching-learning process. Boundaries were to be loosely drawn at first but clearly defined, and they were to be adhered to with the same kind of perseverative quality which Edward demonstrated in his flaunting of human and social values. He was not to be rejected, and his own acts of aggression were to be met by preventive measures as well as controls built into his daily program. Because it was assumed that Edward would aggressively challenge any limits, making it difficult for even the one-to-one relationship to become the instrument of change, the teacher-moms were instructed to seek the constant help of the supervising teacher, as well as the psychologists and consulting psychiatrist. This was done not with the objective of developing an alliance against Edward, but in order to permit preservation of boundaries and communication of values uncluttered by adverse emotional reactions.

On a California Achievement Test (LP), after one year in the project Edward scored as follows:

Reading Vocabulary	2.8	
Reading Comprehension	2.8	
Reading Total		2.8
Arithmetic Reasoning	4.2	
Arithmetic Fundamentals	4.2	
Arithmetic Total		4.2
Mechanics of English	3.4	
Spelling	2.4	
Language Total		2.9
Battery Grade Placement		3.3

It should be noted that these scores were thought to represent his ability under optimal conditions, not his daily level.

As part of a research project, he was subjected to complete psychological testing in September, 1962. On the Wechsler Intelligence Scale for Children he achieved a verbal scale I.Q. of 86, a performance scale I.Q. of 106, and a full scale I.Q. of 95. In the content of the total test material there was still ample evidence of his negativism and manipulativeness. He showed improvement in controls. His projective material showed a sparcity of content and detail. His overall approach to much of the material was superficial and indicative of deliberate attempts at evasion. There was poor psychosexual differentiation. There was extensive evidence of the underlying hostility and aggression that continued to motivate much of his behavior.

In the course of his stay in the project he displayed much of the behavior which had disrupted his regular classroom. He was frequently unresponsive and resistant, using whatever means he could to deflect the teacher-mom from teaching. These means included crying, feigning tiredness, withdrawing by pulling his coat over his head, engaging the teacher-mom in tangential conversations, and complaining about his own difficulties with learning by saying, "The letters keep jumping off the page at me."

Edward's most glaring gap in academic concept-development usually involved reading. He would literally refuse to learn. In arithmetic, he refused to recognize the process of subtraction and would invariably change all subtraction problems to addition. It was always very difficult to establish work patterns with him. On good days, any schedule or sequence of work seemed acceptable. On bad days, nothing worked. His attention span was variable, depending upon his mood. As anticipated, all conventional pedagogical methods seemed unsuccessful in reaching him. Many varied devices were attempted in the teaching of reading. A phonetic approach was used intensively for several months. The teacher-mom and child alternated in reading. The experience-chart method was used with a small measure of success. The Fernald approach was initiated, also with only a small degree of success.

Any attempt to have Edward perform within a group learning situation was invariably doomed to failure. It was only in the one-to-one setting that any academic progress appeared at all. He was frequently surly and sulky. He seemed detached, uncooperative, resistant and unreachable. Mood swings were frequent. He was either blustery or withdrawn. He was extremely sensitive to the intent of any educational program undertaken by his teacher-moms, making every attempt either to terminate the situation or to re-direct the teacher-mom's attention. His behavior ranged from demanding through indifference, aggression, hostility, indiscriminate verbal and physical abusiveness, manipulativeness, suggestibility, tenacity, jealousy—to somatic complaints. He frequently used that façade characterized by a total lack of emotional affect, and initially this defensive wall appeared to be impenetrable. His hyperactivity sometimes presented a problem. It would manifest itself by restlessness and a constant need to get up from his seat. This resulted in his frequently leaving the room and wandering about the hall for short periods of time. He tended to throw small objects, and his internal need to be in motion continually resulted in disruptive behavior. He was often involved in negative acts, such as striking out at another child without apparent cause. As a result of his unpredictable behavior in nonstructured situations, Edward frequently created problems in management. He would throw stones, encourage others to imitate him, run away and hide. When his poorly established boundaries were threatened in any way he would become detached and not allow anyone to break through his hastily erected and protective barrier—and if unsuccessful in this endeavor he would express his loss of control by verbal or physical abusiveness, physically running away or totally refusing to work. When frustrated he would tear up his work, sulk, pick a fight, turn over chairs, and, always, finally find a way to withdraw.

Edward's reaction to his teacher-moms and other adults in general was one of watchful wariness. His response to restrictions imposed by the teacher-moms varied, dependent upon his mood. It was interesting to see how, ultimately, the teacher-in-charge became the authority figure acceptable to Edward. It was almost as if the team approach permitted the teacher-mom to become the instrument of relationship and learning, while the teacher-in-charge became the symbol of limits and controls. Although Edward needed limits in order to function, he made every attempt to alter and redefine them, and in general break them down.

Initially, Edward's reaction to his peer group was one of outright indifference or negativism. He early demonstrated an interest in younger children, toward whom he was most protective. His leadership ability then manifested itself, on both a formal and informal level. They, in turn, looked up to him as a hero, which gave Edward the status he desperately needed. Eventually this was used as an instrument for building relationships by giving him monitorial status. But when participating in either a directed or non-directed activity Edward usually tended to be a disruptive member of the group. With his own age group, when he chose not to be an isolate, he would spend most of his time in passive or peripheral participation.

Educational materials used with Edward included:

Milton Bradley, link-letters and phonics sets
Lippincott phonics books, A–G
Teacher and pupil-made experience charts
Teacher and pupil-made story book, printed on primary typewriter
Weekly Readers, (editions 2 and 3)
Dime store puzzle books
Readers Digest Skill Builders
My First Health Book (in primary type)
Golden Book of Science
Ways of Our Land
Silver-Burdett, *Words We Know* (grade 2 speller)
Heath Science Books
McKee-Harrison language books
Intermediate dictionary
Teacher-made materials for Fernald approach to reading
Noble and Noble handwriting books
Silver-Burdett, *Making Sure of Arithmetic* (grade 2)
Silver-Burdett, *Making Sure of Arithmetic Workbooks*
Supplementary arithmetic materials for Silver-Burdett
Teacher-made and commercial flash cards of number combinations

During the course of his stay in the project many changes took place, in both the educational and social areas. When he first entered he was a non-reader. By May, 1963, his reading total was at a 3.2 level. His arithmetic total was 4.2. His battery grade placement was 3.4. These were certainly below expected levels for his intellectual capacity. However, they contained basic equipment for continued educational progress in the sense that the critical barrier of no equipment had been overcome. But far more important were the obvious changes that took place in this child in attitude, behavior, and affective state. His thought process became more logical and better organized. He began to show good reasoning ability, and the main educational impasse—his refusal to learn—seemed to have been overcome in his general acceptance of the teaching process. A gradual willingness to work appeared. His resistance, in terms of intensity, frequency, and duration, began to melt away. He began to show a positive reaction to the teaching process itself.

There were gradual improvements in Edward's social concepts and attitudes. A social consciousness emerged slowly, with a recognition of cause and effect and related anxiety and verbalizations which reflected his developing awareness. He began to respond positively to strict limits: this was best seen in his relationship with the teacher-in-charge, who often was involved in structuring the overall educational setting. It was found, too, in his acceptance of a written schedule placed before him that required checking off his work as it was accomplished. He slowly became able to perform in modest group learning situations. He accepted and fulfilled obligations in his monitorial status with some of the younger children. More and more he demonstrated a degree of friendliness and even a sense of humor, and, most significantly, anxiety finally emerged as an identifiable factor in his reactive patterns. He demonstrated a growing curiosity and sensitivity to things around him. He was less resentful, less resistant, and not so prone to extreme swings of mood. His manipulative, demanding, and hostile attitude toward others subsided. There was a marked decrease in his need to offer somatic complaints and fatigue as excuses for non-performance. His progress in these areas was viewed as of major importance in altering his patterns of anti-social behavior.

His self-image changed, from one of self-depreciation with a view of himself as an object of rejection, to one indicating signs of beginning acceptance of his own limits and the limits of others. In his own words, he became "a medium boy," who was both "good and bad," "smart and stupid," "afraid and unafraid," "liked and disliked," "weak and strong," "successful and unsuccessful." His emotional responses became more appropriate, and he became more constructively interested in the object and human world around him. What emerged was a more accepting image of himself as a person and as a boy, although there was clear evidence of continuing confusion in many of his concepts.

He showed continuing evidence of establishing better and more extensive control over his own impulses. Although many of his patterns persisted, frequency, duration and intensity diminished. He was more able to channelize his impulses into constructive activity, and as this fact appeared there was an obvious decrease in wanton striking out at others. When Edward became upset he was more prone to show emotion, rather than indiscriminate aggression or withdrawal. In turn, his total affective behavior became more appropriate to the various life situations to which he was exposed. Reasoning with him became an effective technique in reaching and helping him. He himself began to redirect his energy, when frustrated, into an alternative activity at which he might be successful. As opposed to terminating the entire learning situation for the day, as he formerly did, he began to substitute an activity of his own choosing, sometimes tolerating the reintroduction of the difficult subject following the successful completion of his personally selected one. Although his regressive behavior continued to be a problem, it lessened in frequency and degree.

He began to respond to emotional and physical overtures on the part of the adult personnel. He began to be able to tolerate shows of acceptance and affection. He seemed able to relate and interrelate. His indifferent attitude toward the adult world began to disappear. He allowed his inner feelings to reach the surface more often and actually expressed them verbally. Finally he began to look for the adult support that had been so consistently offered him. The remarks of one of his teacher-moms, who had almost given up her own participation in this trying program, summed up the changes in Edward: "In adult-child interpersonal relationships he is a changed boy. If I didn't see it I wouldn't have believed it possible." Associated with all of these changes, of course, was a direct and visible change in his attitude toward his peers, and his acceptance of interaction within the group.

In May, 1963, A California Achievement Test Battery (UP) was administered with the following results, and compared with the September, 1962 scores:

Reading Vocabulary	3.2	(a gain of 4 months)
Reading Comprehension	3.2	(a gain of 4 months)
Reading Total	3.2	(a gain of 4 months)
Arithmetic Reasoning	4.3	(a gain of 1 month)
Arithmetic Fundamentals	4.2	(No change)
Arithmetic Total	4.2	(No change)
Mechanics of English	4.1	(a gain of 7 months)
Spelling	1.9	(a gain of 1 month)
Language Total	3.0	(a gain of 1 month)
Battery Grade Placement	3.4	(a gain of 1 month)

As can be seen, there were small quantitative gains in the educational achievement results. His score now more closely reflected his actual levels of performance on a daily basis. The critical areas of educational change were in his attitude toward school work, and in his slow elimination of outright resistance to the teaching procedure.

Psychological tests administered in May, 1963, reflected many of the changes already described. On the Wechsler Intelligence Scale for Children, he achieved a full scale I.Q. of 104, with a verbal scale I.Q. of 97, and a performance scale I.Q. of 110. His overall attitude, approach to the material, and individual responses seemed greatly improved. His affect was now much more appropriate, and the most outstanding feature of the projective testing was his changed view of the world. He no longer saw it as an empty, cold, sterile place in which to live. The findings confirmed that a major break-through had been accomplished, which apparently allowed him to see his world as having substance instead of being empty and potentially destructive, and populated by indi-viduals capable of giving warmth instead of hurt, rejection, and aggression. There continued to be powerful problem areas. There was distinct confusion in his psychosexual identification. There were many immaturities, but they were not as glaring or significant in the overall psychological constellation. There was manifest anxiety in many areas of his performance, and it was this recognizable existence of anxiety that was thought to be crucial in the project's ability to reach this youngster. He still showed ample evidence of concrete defensive thinking. His controls over impulse still appeared to be poor.

With these changes his movement back into the regular classroom became possible, and was successfully accomplished. In spite of a continuing educational disability which might lead one to question the achievements of the special project, the critical area of change in this child is reflected in his ability to relate appropriately to other human beings. The devastating process of anti-social, pre-delinquent, and incipient psychopathic personality seems to have been halted. In its place, an increased awareness and acceptance of other people appears to have been created. No longer is he toiling to pre-serve his empty fortress. No longer does he seem motivated to indiscriminate attacks on others. Much of his psychic energy is now directed to the critical problems of living. Judging from the results, it is quite conceivable that he has been successfully taught how to live, even though there was only limited success with the teaching of the "three R's."

The story of Edward has within it the yet to be answered question in regard to such children: What is the responsibility of the educator?

5 The Brain-Damaged Child: Case Histories

Introduction

ANOTHER substantial group of children who present extensive problems in training and education do so because of deficits and disturbances in the integrative areas of their functioning. Their disturbances stem from demonstrable biologic and organic causes, which interfere with the maturational sequence and the integrative processes essential to normal development. The resulting lags have extensive effects on the capacity to learn because of perceptual disturbances, problems in impulse control, emotional immaturity, and vulnerability to stress. In many ways, these children resemble the seriously emotionally disturbed children described in the preceding chapter. Their primary problem, however, stems from deficits in internal organization, not from functional disturbance.

Their development, as well as acquisition of function, is

109

insular in nature. They frequently are unable to bridge the gaps between the islands of their own development. The normal educational process, based on the assumption of a functioning whole, becomes an inadequate instrument for teaching these children because they are inadequate instruments for learning within the standardized educational system. The well-established hierarchy of the normal educational sequence is predicated upon the normal sequence of development. You cannot teach a child to run before he can walk, or to read before his perceptual systems are adequately organized and integrated. It is no accident that the educational system begins with the five- and six-year-old. Almost by trial and error and the normal number of successes accompanying this approach, the educator has learned the appropriateness of starting formal learning for most children at this time. But what of the child who achieves this chronology, has the natural intelligence, but is lacking in the organization of his physical, emotional, and intellectual functions? How can these children be taught? Their poor control over impulse results in hyperactivity, distractibility, short attention span—leading to inability to conform to the demands of group learning. The large group teaching-process overwhelms them because of their accompanying emotional immaturity, or they become lost in the crowd with their deficits sometimes not even identified. Their insular development deceives everyone into believing that they are possessed of the capacity to learn and are unwilling to do so. The result is the child's frustration with learning, compounded by the frustration of those responsible for teaching him.

This group of children is commonly classified as the brain-injured. There are a wide variety of such children, defined by the deficit and the nature of their symptoms and malfunction. When motor impairment is the dominant symptom, they are identified as cerebral-palsied children. When they have repeated convulsions, they are called epileptics. When they are plagued by mental subnormality, they are identified as retarded. And when their principal symptom is a disturbance in behavior and the capacity to adjust, they are identified as having organic behavior disorders. These categories are distinguishable, but they present similar constellations of disabilities to plague the child himself and those responsible for his rearing, training, and education.

It is not our intent to discuss the multitude of physical causes leading to this unhappy condition. Rather, it is our purpose to highlight some of the special problems of these children, as their internal deficits influence their behavior and capacity to function.

Almost all of these children grow with a vague awareness of their own inadequacy. Their recognition arises from constant failure, not from an observed correlation between deficit and function. Within the hierarchy of development failure breeds failure, as success breeds success. These children suffer failure without ever being aware of its source. The result is a sense of inadequacy. They become apprehensive and fearful, constantly afraid of new situations because of their conditioning to failure. They become clinging and dependent upon objects and people they know, with the mistaken idea that the familiar will save them from new failure. They are not only clinging in their relationships, but in their overall method of functioning. They would rather repeat a task which they have learned, even to the point of purposelessness, than experience the anxiety of attempting something new. Thus we see the origin and development of their patterns of repetitive behavior, which may be without ultimate purpose beyond permitting them to do what is familiar. There may be other reasons for this perseverative quality but certainly this is a primary cause. Imagine what some of these problems do to compound the difficulties of teaching and learning, where the inherent ingredient is the constant exposure to new and different experiences. Sometimes for no other reason than anxiety these children resist the learning process and reject attempts to teach them.

Another important area of malfunction stems from their own self-image, which is dependent not only upon their accumulated experience in terms of success and failure, but also upon their awareness of self as a functioning whole. All brain-injured children, regardless of the degree or nature of their disability, have some impairment in the formation of their own body- and self-image. If one is composed of parts that do not function easily or well as a whole, this basic experience leads to a concept of fragmentation which dominates one's very fabric. This process can be seen in such testing devices as drawing the human figure, where the organic child literally constructs the body out of parts, pastes it together, and always preserves the most primitive organization of these parts. Or, in terms of his own verbalized concepts of himself, there is a kind of concreteness based on what he can see and feel. It is, indeed, interesting to see this kind of concrete approach pervade every phase of these children's functioning. It almost resembles the cement used to keep bricks together. Their thought process is invariably concrete, and their capacity to approach the abstract is frequently limited, regardless of their innate intelligence. Here again we see the impact of their deficits reinforcing their sense of inadequacy—and yet, also establishing patterns of function which must be recognized as intrinsic to their attempts to function.

Those responsible for helping these children grow must understand the nature of their human fabric. The design of educational devices must be modified to a level compatible with the child's design, because he himself is unable to adapt easily or well to established educational procedures. For instance, so many teaching devices are dependent upon well-established abstract thinking. What of the child who does not have this capacity, or acquires it late? Such children rightfully challenge the educational system—which, itself, has acquired some of the concreteness and perseverative quality of the brain-damaged. The human animal has risen to a position of dominance in the biological world because of its capacity to adapt. Any system designed to train and educate must preserve its own capacity for adaptation—and certainly brain-damaged children pose a problem in adaptation.

A critical problem is impulse control. Regardless of the nature and site of damage or deficit, one result is a disorder of impulse. If one views the central nervous system as a signal center, the number of signals and their nature, frequency, intensity, and range become important to the functioning of the system. These are the quantitative aspects. Similarly, the inherent ability of the system itself to process the impulse in terms of order, sequence, priority, and location, becomes the qualitative aspect. It is easy to see how an organic deficit involving the central nervous system, regardless of its specific nature, has sustained qualitative and quantitative effects on function. The central nervous system, being that part of the body which takes the longest time to mature, by its nature compounds the ultimate effect of these potential variations. Because the evolution of function of the central nervous system is a maturational matter it is apparent that further disturbances in impulse and control may manifest themselves in the course of development. The resulting maturational lags may have widespread significance in respect to the end point of such function, which is human behavior itself.

Think of a simple disorder in the central nervous system of a new born child, and one can readily see how there may be a diffusion into almost every area of behavioral development. So much of behavior is dependent upon proper timing, control, coordination, sequence, and adjustment, it is truly remarkable that the primary impulse problem characteristic of the brain-damaged child does not totally disorganize him. The probable reason rests within the admirable compensatory and adaptable qualities built into all human activity. Indeed, it is in this area that the organic child is most remarkable. If given the opportunity he can, in most instances, compensate for his own deficits. He ultimately will take the disorganizing impulse and channelize it, or compensate for it, in a way that permits him to operate. Here again it is possible to see the constructive aspects of his perseverative nature. By the very character of perseveration, impulse becomes organized and channelized into specific tasks, even though they may be excessively repetitive. The frequently seen rigid and constrictive approach reflects the need for strong, firm controls over an impulse which may be too intense, or so variable that it would disrupt unless handled in this manner.

There is little question that, because of the nature of the problems inherent to the organic process, the time-sequence for the adequate development of pattern and control is prolonged. Thus the maturational process itself is almost always delayed in the organic child. This is usually obvious in his overall immature behavior, function, and attitude. But it is this very slowness that permits internal organization to take place in spite of deficit. It is also this slowness that permits trial and error for the ultimate acquisition of mechanisms designed to circumvent or bridge the intrinsic deficits, and thus finally allow a coalescence into a functioning, whole human being.

But what of an educational system that is geared to chronology, to wholeness, to "normality"? How can this system tolerate a child with basic impulse problems, maturational lags, inadequacies in integrative functioning, and deficiencies in the basic instruments for learning and the group experience? It is obvious that unless this system is able and willing to recognize the intrinsic problems of these children it will have similar problems with the so-called normal, because what has been described for the brain-damaged children has, in many ways, application to all children. Although qualitative differences may not exist in the median of the group, certainly similar quantitative variations can readily be demonstrated. It would seem appropriate for professionals having to do with educating, training, and rearing young children to be aware of, and to learn how to deal with, these problems. The overtly brain-damaged child represents an admirable demonstration unit for the identification of the problems inherent in his own education; at the same time he offers the opportunity for development of techniques adaptable to his needs. By dealing with these children's problems, the learning instrument contained within the child as well as the teaching devices can be welded into a far more efficient, functioning whole, and the concrete, perseverative nature of some of the educational process will be removed forever. The story of Elliott, one of the children in the Elmont special project, highlights many of these problems.

The Brain-Damaged Child

The internal deficits in the brain-damaged child may cause such a wide discrepancy in various areas of function that the child's intellectual potential becomes disguised. His overall behavior may reflect the low points of his development, rather than his median. The result is a degree of impairment that tends to discourage reasonable efforts in behalf of his training and education. This unfortunate set of circumstances was seen in Elliott, a brain-damaged, cerebral-palsied child. He was eight years old when he moved into the Elmont project. Prior to this time he had never been placed in a group beyond the public school kindergarten. He had attended, in his previous classroom placements, on a part-time basis. Several of his placements in other school districts had been terminated because of behavior problems. He had been considered by the community Cerebral Palsy Center, but had been rejected as being too disturbed for their special group.

Following these repeated failures in placement in other communities, it was agreed to admit Elliott to the special project, which he entered in October, 1962.

Elliott truly ran the gamut of the functional and behavioral disabilities seen in brain-damaged children. He had many spastic components in his motor function. His gait was shuffling. He tended to walk and run on his toes, and there was a marked spastic component to the motor function of his lower extremities, with an obvious dragging of his left foot. He was hyperactive and unable to keep his body at rest, so that some part of him was always in movement. He had an obvious visual problem which seemed to have an effect on his spatial orientation. He was nearsighted and unable to bring his eyes into stable focus. Gross and fine motor coordination were poor, with residual, immature, and some abnormal patterns in evidence. He had right-left confusion. Interestingly enough, in spite of the extensive motor involvement, speech patterns were well developed and he had an excellent vocabulary and facility in verbal communication. He spoke almost on an adult level, reflecting his many years of isolation from his peer group and almost constant social contact only with adults.

Elliotts's parents were separated shortly after his birth, and since that time he and his father have been living with the paternal grandparents. Elliott was born six weeks prematurely and spent the first three weeks of his life in the hospital because of low birth weight and excessive neonatal jaundice. He was a hyperactive infant. He spoke early, but walked independently much later than the average child. No really accurate information has been obtained about his developmental landmarks, because the several adults involved in his early rearing were unable to agree on the facts.

This inconsistency in information was reflected in the child-rearing practices. Three parent figures, a generation apart, resulted in considerable differences in approach and attitude toward the many problems Elliott presented. This contributed to some of the child's demanding and aggressive behavior. The paternal grandparents resorted to permissiveness or isolation in attempts to control him. This was mixed with firmness on the part of the father, who found himself in the difficult situation of having to make do under these special living circumstances. Because of other living circumstances during his early childhood, Elliott had little opportunity to experience peer relationships. He spent long periods by himself, which seems to have stimulated a very rich and active fantasy life.

These factors contributed to the behavior problems which led to Elliott's exclusion from various kindergarten placements over a period of several years. The behavior attributed to him was characterized by hyperactivity, negativism, demands for attention, disruption, inability to play with other children, immature and regressed behavior, temper tantrums, hitting, screaming, and throwing things. He was totally unable to participate in group activities, and could only operate either as an isolate or, at best, a peripheral participant. His kindergarten placements had to be terminated because of his decreasing ability to maintain himself in the group setting, and the group's, as well as the teacher's, decreasing ability to tolerate him.

This child's natural history and identified problems set the stage for his programing within the Elmont project. Since Elliott himself related in a very dependent manner to adults this was initially encouraged, in order to build rapidly a relationship with the teacher-moms in which some order and support could be given. This was a simple task in the one-to-one relationship offered by the teacher-mom system. Following this, the entire program was geared directly to his identifiable problems in functioning. Teaching took place with all extraneous stimuli eliminated by placing him, during periods of instruction, in a room by himself with his teacher-mom.

Periods of activity were kept short because of his poor controls and his very limited concentration span. Although heavy reliance on verbal communication was the natural result of the child's own high verbal skills, constant attempts were made to integrate learning by combining auditory, visual, and tactile procedures. From this basic organization of his school program the teacher-mom was encouraged gradually to impose boundaries and limits, and at all times to maintain a consistent attitude toward, and acceptance of, the child. Elliott's program was predicated directly on his functional variations, and it was indeed interesting to see the results.

When he first joined the special project he was at a readiness level in all academic areas. Results of the California Achievement Test (LP) could not be scored on the standardized scale since his raw scores fell well below the base of 1.0 in every area. Psychological testing dramatically revealed the tremendous discrepancies, with a 42-point difference, on the Wechsler Intelligence Scale for Children, between the verbal and performance scale. He achieved a verbal I.Q. of 89, a performance I.Q. of 47, and a full scale I.Q. of 66. The scores were considered minimal, in light of the extensive motor and visual-motor problems, perceptual difficulties, short attention span, impulse problems, and so on. His strongest areas were those of memory and comprehension. It seemed as if a considerable portion of his learning had taken place on the rote level. His projective testing revealed that he had an exceedingly rich imagination, with a heavy fantasy involvement. He seemed to prefer his own imagination or special devices of his own making as a mode of handling any stimulus with which he could not cope. There were many infantile patterns to his responses, and he demonstrated an almost continuous flight of ideas when he responded to some of the test material. His tests indicated a considerable amount of hostility, anxiety, insecurity, and even fragmentation. He handled the material in a very erratic fashion with much perseveration and tangential thinking. It seemed from the results that Elliott had withdrawn, in an attempt to survive in a somewhat threatening reality situation, into his own fantasy-world.

His progress in the project was interesting. Initially his thought processes were characterized by fragmentation, an inability to follow a line of thought, a high degree of distractibility, perseveration, and the blocking-out of unwelcome ideas. He was frequently resistant, and very restless. As previously indicated, he had no measurable educational achievements. He rarely was able to work for more than half the morning, with considerable variation even in this short period of time. He was unable to take the stimulation of group activities. His exposure to the other children in the project so excited him that afterward he was unable to concentrate and frequently became a severe behavior problem.

His attention span when he first came to the project was minimal. He was obsessed with clocks of all kinds. He could not work independently and needed constant supervision, controls and rigid limits. He was found to be highly manipulative and resentful of and toward authority. He was demanding, defiant, aggressive, sometimes verbally abusive, compulsive about time, and blustering in his demeanor. He would resort to somatic complaints, including threats of vomiting, headaches, fatigue. From time to time he demonstrated an overt fearfulness, obvious regressive behavior, and a diffuse kind of anxiety, with vagueness appearing in his general attitude. Episodes of regressive behavior were quite common. From some of his behavior and his own statements, it was obvious that his self-concepts were quite poor. He viewed himself as inadequate and he sometimes resorted to becoming a comic as a cover-up for this sense of inadequacy.

Some of the test results suggested a very primitive, fragmented and even distorted body-image. He seemed unsure of his own physical functioning, the nature of his own body sensations, and his capacity to differentiate in this area. Problems in impulse control were extensive. His ability to control himself was marginal, erratic, and unpredictable. His loss of control frequently took the form of noise-making, during which he imitated clock sounds and other, similar noises. He found release in physical hyperactivity, constant movement in his seat, jumping up, running about in circles, striking out at anyone within range. He seemed to have a special problem in spatial orientation and had difficulty in directing himself from one point to another.

He was impossible to maintain within structured group situations. He was quick to disrupt by a variety of activities. He would push the other children, throw things, scream and draw attention to himself by hysterical laughter. If frustrated by any of the other children he would display a variety of avoidance mechanisms, including fatigue, psychosomatic complaints, perseverative acts, noise-making. Initially he was extremely negative and hostile to all the people in authority. He consistently attempted to test boundaries and limits. Interestingly enough, once he was convinced the limits would be enforced he usually accepted them, but the testing process was an intense one. If subjected to discipline, he might regress or end by involving the supervising adult in a long discussion about the injustices being perpetrated upon him. He rarely demonstrated consideration for the rights of others. Unpredictability was the rule in all his relationships and actions.

Within the period of his first year in the Elmont project there were steady and progressive changes. He settled down and seemed to gratify his immature emotional needs in the one-to-one relationship with his teacher-moms, and his functioning in almost all areas showed a gradual, steady improvement. His memory seemed to improve so that his day-to-day retention of learned material became more consistent. His actual thought process began to show change, as manifested by his greater logic and consistency. Control over impulse became progressively better, and when he was placed on Benadryl there was considerable improvement in his ability to control his physical activity and many of his outbursts. To coincide with this greater ability at physical control, however, his verbal compulsions increased. He talked more and frequently resorted to his compulsive making of clock noises.

In six months Elliott was able to participate in educational programing for the entire morning. His attention span lengthened, his ability to concentrate improved, and his general ability to sustain activity and involvement with relationship showed positive change. He began to tolerate the group. By midyear he had acquired a meaningful relationship with another child, although he still behaved spasmodically in all group activities. He began to accept limits and ceased to react to them.

These changing patterns were quickly reflected in academic achievement. Reevaluation in May, 1963, with the California Achievement Test (LP) showed the following scores, as compared with September, 1962:

Reading Vocabulary	2.2	(a gain of more than 2 years)
Reading Comprehension	0	
Reading Total	1.1	(a gain of more than 1 year)
Arithmetic Reasoning	1.5	(a gain of 1½ years)
Arithmetic Fundamentals	1.7	(a gain of more than 1½ years)
Arithmetic Total	1.6	(a gain of more than 1½ years)
Mechanics of English	2.2	(a gain of 2 years)
Spelling	2.8	(a gain of 2½ years)
Language Total	2.5	(a gain of 2½ years)
Battery Grade Placement	1.8	(a gain of about 2 years)

What appears most dramatic, educationally, is Elliott's movement from complete non-academic functioning to an academic achievement level close to second grade in all areas except reading comprehension. This occurred despite extensive problems and continuing evidence of his own internal deficits.

The teaching devices used to obtain these results were highly individualized to accommodate Elliott's needs. At the outset it was obvious that he could benefit from instruction on a one-to-one basis only if all peripheral stimuli were filtered out. This was done not only by teaching him in a room by himself, but by facing him directly into a corner. Because of his severe visual-motor perceptual problems his academics were presented to him in combination with tactile, kinesthetic, auditory, oral, and rote methods. All work was presented in simple units, with clearly defined boundaries. Initially Elliott could recognize letters and words in upper case print only: his pre-primers and workbooks were retyped in upper case. After four months of this approach, when Elliott had mastered the upper case print, matching books were presented with regular print. This device appeared to have been successful because he continued to learn to read with conventional print. His obsession with clocks of all kinds was deliberately used as an instrument of motivation, incentive, reward, punishment, and teaching. He was never permitted to work independently, since he was unable to sustain any effort on his own. He needed constant supervision and controls, and rigid limits.

The educational material used with Elliott included the following:

S.R.A. *Learning to Think Series* (Red, Blue, Green books)
Ginn & Co. pre-primer and workbooks, retyped in upper case
Ginn & Co. pre-primer and workbooks
Games We Play
Fun with Tom and Betty
"*I See*" Book
Ginn & Co. pre-primer flash cards
Weekly Surprise
Weekly Reader (edition 1)

Golden Dictionary
Making Sure of Arithmetic, Book 1
Milton Bradley, *Judy Clock*
Creative, *Take-Apart Clock*
Metronome
Heavy crayons, pencils
Easel
Flannel board
Milton Bradley, Flannel board letters and numbers

Elliott was given another battery of psychological tests in May, 1963. On the Weschsler Intelligence Scale for Children he achieved a verbal scale I.Q. of 91, performance scale I.Q. of 47, and full scale I.Q. of 67. There was no significant difference in the test results, as compared with the previous fall. Within the projective material, however, there was ample evidence of changes taking place in his personality structure to reflect the changes in his behavior. He seemed much more reality-oriented and no longer showed an excessive tendency to withdraw into fantasy, although he still demonstrated a very rich imagination. He seemed preoccupied with the world as hostile, threatening, and unpredictable, but his overall attitude reflected a willingness to attempt to cope with it. His progress in the one-to-one relationship seemed to have increased his awareness of his environment, but with it there was some obvious increase in anxiety. Problems in impulse control were still very much in evidence. Fragmentation of thought process continued to be a problem, but there was also an emerging concreteness.

Elliott has continued in the special project for two full years. In spite of the contradiction of his intellectual quotients (in the educable retarded range), he has continued to show academic progress comparable to his innate intelligence, which is more accurately reflected in his verbal performance. It is doubtful that Elliott could have begun to approach this level of academic progress in anything but the one-to-one teaching process. When he came to the project he was already entrenched in his own system of failure, not only in the educational areas but in his social and emotional existence. The substitution of success for failure was the project's gift to Elliott. In turn, his gift to the educational system was an increased awareness in the system of the differences within a child as well as between children. No longer can children be routinely categorized according to their chronological age or their intellectual testing. There is little question that Elliott will continue to need specialized programing. However, with the advances that he continues to make, his movement into the world of his contemporaries seems assured. Brain-damaged children, more than any other group, demonstrate the therapeutic values of successfully applied educational techniques.

The Child Who Could Not Be Rescued

The educational process cannot always be adapted. Problems within and around a child may sometimes be of a nature and magnitude that disrupt all constructive effort. In such instances identification may be the only meaningful instrument available to help. With identification of the problems, the educator is at least able to modify his approach in recognition of the existence of forces greater than those he can deal with. Thus he becomes better equipped to involve himself in programing—the ultimate design of which becomes a contribution to the child, even if it does lead to exclusion or institutional care. There is little question that under certain circumstances the formal, organized educational program is relatively insignificant to the child's overall life experience. No matter what the educator may attempt, sometimes the real solution rests in the resolution of difficulties in areas other than education.

Such is the story of Ted, who at the time of writing has

spent almost a third of his life in a state hospital. His erratic, unpredictable behavior brought him to the attention of the school administration almost as soon as he entered the system. His impulsivity, uncontrollable temper outbursts, anti-social behavior, and inability to perform as a member of the group without being threatening and destructive, resulted in his being referred for psychological evaluation during his first month in kindergarten. By the middle of the kindergarten year, Ted's parents reluctantly agreed to accept referral to the local mental health clinic for psychiatric evaluation. The referral resulted in a recommendation for retention in kindergarten for another year because of his lack of readiness to cope with a more formally structured class. He was also placed on medication and seemed to function more successfully with it. But in the course of his repeating kindergarten his mother discontinued medication, and his behavioral problems returned to such a degree that he could no longer be contained in the classroom. At this point he was excluded.

He was subsequently moved into the special project. On entering, in 1959, he was severely hyperactive and highly distractible. He was given to uncontrollable outbursts of temper. His gross and fine motor coordination were poor. He had a severe problem with vision, correctible with glasses to 20/200 in one eye and 20/40 in the other. He was an awkward, erratic child, but frequently demonstrative of emotion. He deliberately employed displays of affection which were not always sincere, but which at times had been seductively successful. When Ted entered the project he was seven-and-a-half. Academically he was on a readiness level in reading, a low first grade level in arithmetic, and a first grade level in oral language ability. At that time psychological testing data available were incomplete because of his uncooperativeness and intrinsic problems in control, with erratic, unpredictable functioning. The school psychologist estimated his I.Q. at approximately 85 from partially completed testing.

For a combination of reasons it was impossible to maintain Ted within the special project. His outbursts sometimes were violent. Efforts of the teacher-moms and professional staff had to be directed at simple containment. His mother was completely uncooperative in maintaining Ted on the pre-scribed medication, even though it made a tangible difference in his behavior and ability to function. (It was learned sub-sequently that Ted's mother had the unshakable conviction that the medicine was harmful and might even poison her child.) Ted was excluded and placed on home teaching. Even this was short-lived because of the lack of cooperation within the home. His mother contended that she could better teach him herself, and at this point all educational services from the school district were reluctantly discontinued. Ted's behavior grew so destructive within the home that the mother accepted the recommendation of the mental health clinic and com-mitted Ted to a state hospital. Because of parental concern and discontent with the services offered by the state hospital, however, Ted was shortly discharged. His behavior at home remained so disruptive that he was readmitted to the hospital after a very short period of time. He remained at the hospital for a two-year period, when he was again discharged to his home. It was at this time that he was readmitted to the Elmont special project, in which he was programed for a period of three months. At the end of this time, although he seemed to be making progress within the project, problems in interaction within the home led to recommitment by his mother to the state hospital.

Ted's background was indeed a complicated one. His mother had first been married at fifteen or sixteen. In the five years of this marriage she had two children who were now grown and out of the home. The marriage terminated in divorce. Subsequently she had a third child, a girl, out of wedlock. She then married yet another man. She had another daughter from this union and was three months pregnant with

Ted when she discovered that she was involved in a bigamous relationship and had the marriage annulled. She subsequently married a third time and had another daughter. Her current marriage is a stormy one and has been complicated by separations. The home situation remains generally unsettled, with other adults occasionally within the home.

Review of Ted's developmental history revealed many outstanding and possibly critical factors contributing to his basic disorganization and vulnerability. His mother had had a number of miscarriages. She stained and had episodic hemorrhages all during her pregnancy with Ted. At one point she had to be hospitalized and given transfusions. Her pregnancy with Ted terminated prematurely with twin births in the seventh month. The birthweight of the twins was approximately two pounds each. Ted's twin lived for four months and died from a reported boric-acid poisoning. Ted was also reported to have been affected but he recovered. He subsequently had meningitis, with high fever, and again recovered.

The developmental landmarks that could be obtained were irregular but within the normal range. He was reported to have walked by ten months. He began speaking simple words by two years. He was bowel trained by three. He continued to wet well into his seventh year. He was a body-rocker from early infancy. He was always hyperactive and difficult to control. Thus his developmental history reveals a most heroic struggle, starting from the point of conception, for survival. His prenatal existence was replete with events including induced and spontaneous hemorrhage, maternal illness, prematurity, and twinning. His postnatal existence was complicated early by drug toxicity, infection, poor patterning, and extensive maturational disturbances and lags.

At the community mental health clinic the opinion was offered that Ted was the victim of diffuse damage to his central nervous system, with a diagnosis of chronic brain syndrome and a conduct disorder. Subsequent neurological evaluation revealed an abnormal electroencephalogram compatible with a further diagnosis of epileptic seizure patterns of a petit-mal nature. The possibility was considered that some of his outbursts were epileptic equivalents.

It is significant to note that Ted always showed improved behavior while on medication. It was impossible to sustain any medical drug program, however, because of the mother's concern about the use of drugs and her unwillingness to administer them on any sustained basis.

At the time of Ted's readmission to the special project, at the age of nine, he was untestable academically. It was estimated that he could operate, generally, on a first grade level except in oral language ability, in which he was estimated to be at third to fourth grade level. He did participate in a psychological test which required several sessions for its completion. On the Wechsler Intelligence Scale for Children he achieved a verbal I.Q. of 81, a performance I.Q. of 62, and a full scale I.Q. of 70. There was a significant spread of 26 points between the verbal and the performance I.Q. His performance was replete with immaturities and obvious maturational lags. Much of his projective material indicated a kind of negativism colored by a sad, pessimistic quality, as well as extreme feelings of hostility and anxiety. His fantasy reflected a view of the world as hostile and threatening.

Within the project Ted was defiant, aggressive, and highly manipulative with both people and situations. He frequently displayed insincere affection in order to win people over and get what he wanted. He tested limits almost constantly. He spat, kicked, and cursed when out of control. His thought processes seemed irrational and at times disconnected. In many instances his responses were inappropriate. His behavior was characterized by extreme and rapid mood swings ranging from overt hostility to extreme tenderness. His ability to focus on any specific task was limited. He deliberately lied to gain his own ends. His ever ready profuse apologies, which were so obviously insincere, were calculated and premeditated. His overall performance was colored by extreme restlessness, distractibility, and hyperactivity, coupled with a marked lack of day-to-day retention of what was learned on the previous day.

As time progressed, Ted's thought processes and behavior seemed to deteriorate, and he became increasingly uncooperative and belligerent. These moods finally predominated. His unwillingness to work was an increasing problem. It became apparent that Ted needed help in developing even very primary educational concepts. At that time it was felt that these deficits were directly attributable to a basic lack of exposure to academic situations, as well as to his manifest resistance to learning.

Because of Ted's complicated history, project goals were limited to very specific objectives. The foremost was to help this child achieve a transition into a home, school, and community living experience. From his behavior and general level of functioning, it was obvious that educational goals would be totally unrealistic. By his attitudes and behavior Ted projected a set of personal values unrelated to any meaningful functioning within a school situation. It was felt that unless such values could be introduced, attempts at formal education would have little meaning. Ted's operation within relationships had also become so obviously self-centered that it was considered vital to establish a climate for interaction and the development of new values. No real communication of educational techniques would otherwise be possible. Ted's own set of values for living by impulse, seduction, and aggression had to be met head-on. Finally, it was recognized that no instrument for educational learning existed within this child. All teaching devices would have to be primary ones despite his innate intelligence, which was, however, beginning to show the ravages of non-learning.

Early in Ted's stay in the project it was found that he

could participate at his best at mid-morning. On arrival he appeared overstimulated and disorganized. As dismissal time drew near he became anxious. Any academic work, therefore, had to be scheduled around mid-morning for optimum attention. He was most difficult on days when he did not get his medication. At best his attention span was very short, and five-minute work periods were all that could profitably be scheduled. These had to be interspersed with feedings, games, taking a walk, talking. It was evident that conventional teaching devices would be uniformly unsuccessful. He responded best to bribery. Praise and encouragement proved meaningless. Criticism or any kind of punishment destroyed the learning situation entirely.

A teaching program, therefore, was embarked upon involving the extensive use of food, candy, and cookies as incentives and rewards. Because of his severe visual handicap and his total lack of interest in conventional reading material, the teaching of reading was attempted by the use of rote songs which Ted knew, and the words of which he could follow on a typewritten sheet. Another method was to have Ted tell a story to the tape recorder. This story was then typed on a primary typewriter. The following day Ted listened to his tape while following the printed words. He also enjoyed composing lists of rhyming words, which the teacher-mom would write on the blackboard for Ted to read back. To teach counting he and the teacher-mom would play dominoes, checkers, and store, using toy money. Other materials included:

Variously colored toy cars
Milton Bradley, *Number-ite*
Housekeeping toys
Calendar
Abacus
Story-telling records and record player
Piano

Clocks
Milton Bradley, *Judy Clock*
Creative, *Clock Puzzle*
Weekly Surprise
Weekly Reader (edition 1)
Golden Book of Science
Ginn and Co. pre-primer and programed primer, with workbooks

Ted spent only two months at the project during his second stay, at the end of which he appeared to be making some academic progress, unmeasurable though it was. At the end of this time his mother had him recommitted to the state hospital. This move was unrelated to any of the problems connected with the project itself, but was precipitated by problems within the home and neighborhood. Ted had developed a predilection for getting into and trying to start cars. This habit was judged uncontrollable and dangerous by his mother and the supervising clinic. Within the project itself it was the consensus that he could have been contained with medication and that there was beginning evidence of positive change. This suggested that further improvement might have been anticipated had Ted continued in the project.

Our limited contact with this child, and our observation of his patterns of functioning, provided an opportunity to note how deeply a child's behavior can reflect his intrinsic problems of development as well as the interaction between him and his environment. On initial contact Ted almost always presented the picture of a friendly, talkative, and pleasant youngster. This affect could be maintained as long as the situation in which he found himself made no taxing demands, allowed him to function without stress, and permitted him to maintain control. When any of these conditions varied there would be a transformation to an openly defiant, hostile, sulky, sullen, and generally unpleasant attitude. Such exaggerated mood swings were most typical of Ted's functioning. He could be bright and gay, then become withdrawn and sullen. He could swing from ingratiating to defiant, from loving to completely rejecting. Terms of endearment could be replaced with verbal abusiveness. Displays of dependent, clinging behavior could change to aggressive, physical assault. His distrust of the world, and his view of it as hostile, punitive, and threatening, was evident in every aspect of his behavior. He functioned in "con-man" fashion. He was insincere, highly manipulative, and capable of anything he felt would gain his ends.

His own image of himself was totally contradictory. He openly looked for and encouraged remarks to reinforce a flattering picture of himself, and this obviously gave him pleasure and satisfaction. He saw himself as an entertainer and was "on stage" every possible minute. He frequently imitated rock and roll singers and comedians. On the other hand he directly condemned himself as bad, and found it almost impossible to believe that people liked him, let alone loved him. He often referred to himself as "stupid," and reacted with incredulity to protestations against this idea.

He clearly reflected problems in psychosexual identification. In our earlier experience with him he had actively expressed the desire to be a girl. This had disappeared by the time of our second contact, but from the material that could be obtained it was apparent that a distinctive and well-entrenched identity for himself was not established. Some of this disorganization poured over into his fragmented body-image concepts, which were demonstrated in his figure drawings. Legs came from the head. Only the hair differentiated the female figure from the male. His immature and distorted reproductions were commensurate with his retarded level of performance, but they also reflected the readily identifiable organic components which were basic to his disturbance in functioning. At the same time his immature reproductions, which lacked details that differentiated between male and female, conflicted with his vivid and accurately verbalized descriptions of male and female anatomy and how the sexual act is consummated.

He verbalized bodily preoccupation, particularly in the sexual areas. His precocity here was stimulated by reported observations of the primal scene and reported exposures to extensive discussions elsewhere relating to sexual matters. This apparent incongruity is in keeping with the unevenness and unpredictability of his general functioning and of his life experience.

Ted's impulsivity and poor controls were certainly the major source of persistent problems. He could tolerate little or no frustration, and almost always responded negatively to attempts at setting the limits he so desperately needed. His temper tantrums continued to be frequent, and included ranting, raving, and pushing over furniture. On occasion he employed physical attacks on the teacher-moms. He would run and hide in an attempt to avoid the imposition of controls or the demand for work. When his behavior was too distracting, or detrimental to the other members of the group, it would be necessary to take Ted home. Even the mention of this was upsetting to him, but the actuality called forth hysterical crying, pleas for mercy, and meaningless promises to behave. Such uncontrolled and uncontrollable behavior typified much of his daily mode of living during his short stay in the special project.

Ted's relationship with the teacher-moms reflected his overall manipulative nature. He constantly tested his relationships with everyone in an attempt to evaluate just how far he could go. He tried to determine the vulnerable points of each, with the intention of attacking in that area or using his knowledge to bargain when the opportunity arose. He recognized his ability to be threatening and utilized it to the fullest extent. He was aware of his ability to shock, and took obvious pleasure in vulgar conversation and comments deliberately aimed at eliciting shock reactions. He made a studied effort to pressure the teacher-moms into anxiety or to make them angry enough to lose control. He enjoyed their agitation and consternation. Unfortunately, Ted interpreted kindness and patience as weakness. His insincere attitude and his inability to respond positively to the many overtures and unceasing efforts to reach him made the general job of working with him a heart-breaking one for the teacher-moms. Every day became a battle of wills and wits because of Ted's own approach.

In contrast, he made only fleeting efforts to relate to his own peers. He was literally disinterested in them. He showed no enjoyment in playing with them, and could not operate as a member of any team. He therefore avoided all organized play activity. He did not even enjoy spectator status, but would rather roam off by himself. He tended by choice to isolate himself from the other children. Competition for attention sometimes resulted in aggressive acts, but more frequently took the form of a simple temper tantrum. His generally provocative behavior resulted in his becoming the butt of the group. They frequently made fun of him and deliberately tried to upset him by calling him "four eyes" or "baby."

We can see that Ted's anti-social attitude and behavior reflected many of his problems; they seemed to result from his never having received the love and acceptance that he so desperately wanted. To the foundation of his own internal problems and vulnerability he added the anxieties, aggressive tendencies, and disorganization reflected in his life situation. These negative qualities became incorporated into his behavioral pattern. It is truly interesting to note that in the two months of contact with him his anxiety seemed to increase with a growing awareness of his faulty functioning, and with an awareness of his inadequate physical and emotional equipment for coping with life.

It would seem obvious that Ted's problems must inhibit

any learning process other than one which blended with his well-entrenched distortions. Certainly, it would be impossible to reach this kind of child in any group educational situation. His pattern of disruption and destruction of relationships, even the most carefully constructed personal relationships, would interfere with any group. The only device that might conceivably succeed would be one which took into account his own mechanisms and patterns of functioning, and this approach can only be constructed within a one-to-one relationship. Even with this opportunity, Ted's disturbances were of a magnitude that could not be adequately compensated for.

Ted is one individual who by nature and nurture was robbed of the basic equipment for constructive learning. In this case the educator can only recognize his inability to alter the course. But he should be able to develop a methodology for appropriate identification, and thus make a maximum contribution to programing and planning for all the children who are his responsibility. Perhaps these unsolved problems make a contribution by continuing to present the challenge they do. Institutionalization as a solution eliminates the challenge. New ideas which might help develop techniques by which the educational instrument—the child—might be altered, and the educational process enriched for all children, could become the result of attempts to work with children like Ted.

6 The Teacher-Mom

THE mental health team of educator, psychologist, and psychiatrist has been expanded, in the Elmont project, to include the teacher-mom as the fourth member. She is the operational extension of the educator, the school psychologist, and the consulting psychiatrist. She is the instrument by which their professional skills are implemented and shared by more children than could benefit otherwise. She complements their skills by bringing to the children her own professional skills as mother and successful child-rearer. She is essential, and, to a great degree, the key to the success achieved.

What of the teacher-moms? How has participation in this project, and sustained effort with seriously disturbed children, affected them personally: has it brought about changes in the management of their homes, of their relationships with their children, husbands, and friends? And what is it that motivates them?

To find the answers to these questions ten teacher-moms were interviewed in depth, as were seven of their husbands. Three of these teacher-moms started when the project began, two have worked in it for two and a half years, three for one and a half years, and two were completing their first year. Four were asked by one of the authors to work in the project, three heard about it at a P.T.A. meeting, three heard about it through other teacher-moms or friends of teacher-moms.

Their initial reactions to the project had been highly favorable. After working in the project they were even more enthusiastic. Seven of ten had, for a number of years, been quite active in religious or community affairs. Three had not. Why were they working in this project? One teacher-mom said she thought it was a "challenge." Another said that when she was asked by one of the authors to help, and understood the plight of the children involved, she "just couldn't say no." Three others pointed out that they had been working in various organizations for a number of years, serving on committees and the like, until they had gotten so they "hated meetings." The idea of giving direct service to a child, particularly a handicapped child, appealed to them. Three others stated they were interested in "these children," and could easily afford the time. Two others thought such work would be "helpful."

The reactions of the seven husbands to their wives' recruitment for the project were equally good. They were pleased that their wives had volunteered. All said they preferred to have their wives give free time to constructive community service rather than spend it all socializing, playing cards and staying at home, or, as one man put it, "becoming a slave to housework." All stated their wives seemed to derive much pleasure and satisfaction from working with disturbed children. One, whose wife was in her second year with the project, questioned whether his wife should continue the next year; he felt that after two years she should "get away from it for a while because it takes so much out of her."

Their work in the project apparently had little effect on family routines. All ten teacher-moms and all seven husbands said it had not changed or interrupted the rhythms of their households. All the teacher-moms and all the husbands said their children were proud of what their mothers were doing. Seven of the ten teacher-moms and six of the seven fathers pointed out that, as an outgrowth of the project, they had a better understanding of their own children's behavior and had become more patient. All agreed they had a better understanding of the disturbed child and had developed a greater awareness of community mental health problems and mental health needs in general.

The teacher-moms derive great pleasure and satisfaction from seeing children improve, but have no illusions about what they are attempting to do. When they were asked what they found most difficult about their work, six replied, "Nothing in particular." One mentioned the repetitiveness and "back-teaching" in the presentation of academic material to the child with whom she was working. Another had some concern about her role when the child with whom she was working became "upset." Another found the paper work distasteful. Another found it difficult in the morning: "The physical pressure of getting to the project by 9:00 A.M."

All the teacher-moms indicated that relatives, friends, and neighbors with whom they discussed the project reacted with interest and concern and displayed positive feelings about it.

All teacher-moms felt strongly that this kind of service to children is the responsibility of school districts, whether in the structure of the Elmont project or some other. They would not hesitate to recommend the initiation of a similar project to other school districts. All felt the state should be making a greater effort on behalf of the troubled child. Some felt the federal government should help by financing research projects and taking a more active part in the recruitment and training of special education personnel.

Generally, they felt the children would benefit more from the Elmont approach than from institutionalization. Several nonetheless pointed out that an exception might be the child whose home situation is so negative that it militates strongly against progress. As the case histories suggest, however, even those children with families with overriding and serious pathology make substantial progress in the special project.

A word about the teacher-moms as individuals. Who are they? One is a sixty-year-old grandmother who travels on her days at the project on two buses and spends one and a half hours commuting each way. Another is the wife of a prosperous dentist with two teenage boys and a grade school girl of her own. A third is the wife of a busy physician and mother of two grade school boys. Another is the wife of one of the authors, with two grown children, one married, another in college. Another is a mother with four grown children. Her circumstances require her to work, which she does at a local nursery school, but with the stipulation that she be free for her mornings at the project. Another is a mother of three, one of whom is in an institution for mental retardates. Another is a nurse by profession, with grown children. Another is a mother with a brain-damaged daughter of her own in one of the regular classes in the Elmont district. She has recently completed courses for certification in special education and is now working in that field. Another is a mother with a physical education background who also went back to college to complete her courses. She is now working as a supplementary teacher in special education with emotionally disturbed children in regular classes in the Elmont district. Another is the wife of a relatively prosperous manufacturer who has a college-age daughter and who comes to the project from a neighboring town. Another is the wife of a professional musician and music teacher with children of grade school age. In short, the teacher-moms represent a cross-section of the mothers found in almost any community.

Their devotion to the project has resulted in an attendance record better than that of the paid professional staff of the Elmont district. (This does not detract from the Elmont teaching staff, which has a superior record of attendance.) There have been a number of instances when teacher-moms have come in to the project on scheduled days although their own children, or their husbands, have been home ill. One even hired a sitter when her own child was ill, so that her project child would not have his schedule interrupted or his relationship with her jeopardized.

In religious background there are Protestants, Catholics, and Jews among the teacher-moms. Perhaps in religious belief lies a part of their motivation. Surely a common denominator among the three is belief in the integrity of the individual and charity for neighbor. The authors claim no extraordinary influence with the Good Lord but they can't help feeling that, if there is a Hereafter, the contribution of these women will not go unnoticed, or unrewarded.

One aid to sustaining their efforts has been their sociability. Some have a bowling club. Others have parties at their swimming pools. Others spend evenings together visiting or going out to dinner. The Elmont Kiwanis Club annually presents a dinner for the teacher-moms and their husbands, and awards them certificates for outstanding service to the youth of the community. The club also presents modest gifts when the teacher-moms go on "tenure"—that is, when they have completed three years with the project. This is a gala night at which one of the authors thanks them publicly with their husbands present, and individually makes the presentations.

All of this, together with the way they are accepted as professionals at the project, has produced a kind of status.

They are a group apart and generally looked up to by the whole community.

Perhaps more important, however, is the fact that from the beginning the approach has been: "There is a job to be done," not "Please help us," as is so often the case when women are asked to volunteer. It makes a difference. The original teacher-moms were secured by invitation of the school administrator to do a job the schools would not be in a position to do without them. This, perhaps, created a vested interest in the project from the beginning and may account, in part, for their faithfulness to duty and their remarkable attendance: for if they were not conscientious about their jobs they would sacrifice themselves as well as the project.

The unusually successful experience the Elmont project has had with teacher-mom volunteers, which is unlike the experience of most agencies with volunteers, may also be due in part to influences evolving out of our present culture. Since the "emancipation" of women most of us expect women to be "more" than "slaves to housework." But society has provided few opportunities for "more" in a way compatible with their basic responsibility as homemakers. Their children grow up, but they still have some responsibility because the basic unit of society is the family and the home; still, they are expected to move out a bit and do something "more." In almost no community, however, is there room for women to make use of their skills as professional child-rearers. The teacher-mom role provides this opportunity. It mobilizes the basic assets of integrity as a person, educational background, and child-rearing experience, and puts them to work in such a way that all are exploited in helping a disturbed child. It is a chance for a woman to fulfill her female role in a satisfying, graceful manner. It is an opportunity for her to attain the heroic. This is important, for there is some of the heroic in each of us. The teacher-mom's satisfaction then, probably comes not so much from the device—the Elmont project—as from the fulfillment of her own self-image. The project plays to her strengths, not her weaknesses.

The community, then, has a responsibility. If it says "more" is expected of women, it has a duty to provide them with opportunities to fulfill this expectation. Generally, what is offered women is an opportunity to help in fund-raising, hospital volunteer work, sometimes innocuous club projects. Very often, as volunteers, they wind up working under people they are above—standing around waiting to be called for some task that requires little more than physical energy, and the value of which can sometimes be questioned. They become time-killers as volunteers, and it is no wonder agencies generally place little reliance on them.

The Elmont project for troubled children provides an opportunity for selected women to become teacher-moms. There is a great qualitative difference between the teacher-mom, working day after day with a disturbed child, and most volunteers. The teacher-mom is a functional worker. She is an extension of the professional educator, the psychologist, and the psychiatrist. She is the fourth member of the team, with a responsibility unlike, but in many ways like, the professionals. All of her skills are called upon. There is no blueprint. Helping the troubled child has to be accomplished by the trial and error approach, with good judgment and intuition. These women are masters at the trial and error approach because this is the way we grow up. It is the way we live. It is how we raise our children.

This again raises the point of teacher-mom rewards. Perhaps the process discussed above leads to the same rewards most professionals and scientists get: the establishment of self-identity as a result of organizing and implementing ideas; the achievement of success at the end of trial and error; a breakthrough, at the end of many trials and errors, when a successful trial is made. This in turn leads to a group identity based on the natural end-point of the emancipation of women, the expectation of the culture that their freedom requires them to accept a corresponding responsibility. The teacher-moms may have achieved a neatly balanced role within the context of our culture: a merger of mother and homemaker, the utilization of mother skills in a part-time career. Most career women must be willing to give up something for their careers. Most housewives must be willing to give up something to be housewives. This makes for conflict in either woman. The teacher-mom gives up nothing basic. She has the best of being a housewife and mother, and the best of a career.

The teacher-mom emerged as one of the critical forces in the success of the program. In the initial conception, the teacher-mom was to make possible the one-to-one relationship deemed essential for the education and training of these disturbed children. It was soon evident, however, that these women were bringing something quite unique and special to the one-to-one relationship. By design, they had been given very little indoctrination and training for the task. This was done, in part, in order to encourage a maximum degree of participation and to avoid the passive role that so frequently becomes the part of the volunteer worker. It was also done because the professional team was itself uncertain of the specific needs of the children. It was felt that each program would have to emerge from experience with the individual child and his reaction to the relationship offered him. It soon became evident, under these conditions, that the teacher-moms had introduced a special ingredient of their own which had not been anticipated.

Most of the women had been chosen on the basis of their extensive training in the job of mother. Since all had reared their own children, it was felt they had the basic experience to deal with most of the problems which might arise. Part of the fundamental philosophy was to consider the troubled children first as children. With it came the attitude that disturbed behavior must be viewed as an exaggerated state of normal behavior, or inappropriate behavior because of immaturity, for a particular child. With these inherent assumptions, the teacher-mom, as a result of her own background, was considered capable of handling the qualitative aspects of most of the expected disturbed behavior. The quantitative aspects, which are always excessive in the disturbed child, were to be handled by the nature of the program, its structure, and the professional team. In the educational areas, it fell to the trained primary grade teacher in charge of the program to structure and select the teaching devices to be used with each child. Since these varied considerably from one youngster to another, each educational instrument was explained as it was attempted and applied. This emerged as a successful system for teaching, but did not seem to be the critical factor in learning for most of the children. The relationship which developed between teacher-mom and child seemed to become the critical instrument for communication: first on a feeling level, then on a relationship level, then on a learning level, and finally on a teaching level. This cycle became a recurrent one with many of the children. Most important, the cycle was unrelated to the individual diagnosis or specific disabilities of the children. It was the teacher-mom who seemed to be able to bring the necessary ingredients, irrespective of diagnosis, to assure the development of meaningful and appropriate feelings and relationships. Once these were established, the learning and teaching process became possible in a far more effective manner than ever before.

As seen from the case histories, most of the children had some degree of affective disturbance which served to distort their reactive patterns and with it their relationships with other human beings. Their emotional and social values and symbols reflected this well-established disturbance, and in turn affected all of their feelings and relationships. Since the teacher-moms had been conditioned by their experience to feelings and relationships with their own children, they seemed not to compound the child's distortions. Frequently they were able to correct, modify, and change some of the values and symbols of the child with whom they were working. It was here that the teacher-mom earned her title of teacher-mom, and took on the particular and distinctive role that had not been anticipated or planned. It didn't seem to matter what the particular personality of the teacher-mom was. Encouraged to do what came naturally, she seemed to be able to call upon her own accumulated experience in child-rearing to develop appropriate feeling and relationship reactions with the child in the special project. As she did this, she gave the child a contrasting set of experiences, from which new values might emerge. Since this was done in a natural and persistently repetitive manner (which was strongly encouraged), the disturbed child, in many instances for the first time, had the opportunity to select successful modes of functioning in feeling and relationship. Thus, a system of positive gain was introduced into the life experience of children whose own systems of gains had led them down the pathway of isolation, rejection, anxiety, and withdrawal. With these new modes to be experienced, it seemed natural for many to reach out for the new experiences and experiment with the possible gains. And this they did—some to the point where they gave up their abnormal defenses for living and became ready and eager for the process of learning.

And learn they did. The majority of the children in the project showed educational gains that exceeded the normal expected rate of learning for a given time period, and in almost all instances the children showed changes in their affective states with modification of their functioning. Many positive elements in relationships with peers and adults seemed to appear. From a technical point of view, it became obvious that a device had been hit upon which incorporated therapeutic principles into the teacher-child relationship. Since all relationship of a positive nature is therapeutic, it is safe to say that the teacher-moms were never *endowed* with a therapeutic role. Their responsibility was to react appropriately and consistently, and to be an extension of the trained teacher in order to make possible a one-to-one teaching situation.

In reviewing the behavior and response systems of the children, it is obvious that each of the children brought his own well-established patterns of personality into the relationship structured by the teacher-mom. It was this structure which then made it possible for the teacher-mom to deal directly with the child's problems on a one-to-one basis. Perhaps it was this structure which permitted change to take place within the reactive patterns of the child.

It is important to stress that the teacher-mom was not left completely to her own resources in handling all the behavior patterns which emerged. When particular difficulties developed she could discuss them with members of the professional team. There were always other teacher-moms on the scene and here, too, they offered each other considerable support and the opportunity to evolve collective decisions. The security of this kind of adult group made for a greater sense of certainty, and the sounding-board provided by group interaction encouraged the rapid evolution of techniques.

Since the teacher-moms were encouraged to seek out a one-to-one relationship they were unable to avoid the particular emotional demands and defenses of the child. This transference was encouraged and even stimulated by the nature of the relationship. The interaction made the three hours each day a laboratory of human experience for the children. For the most part they were then exposed to a response system considerably different from the one they knew at home. Possibly this interaction served as the catalyst for the gradual changes observed.

Since this process was identified relatively early in the history of the project, the professional staff attempted to develop a system for ongoing identification and a method for handling problems as they arose. The teacher-in-charge became a once-removed observation post, where the problems of interaction between child and teacher-mom could be constantly inspected. One of the school psychologists, who was familiar with each of the children, visited the project almost daily and served as a second counter-balance. Problems were brought to the attention of the consulting psychiatrist on a monthly basis and by telephone in emergencies. Surrounded in this manner, and supported by the total team, the teacher-mom was able to work with a greater sense of certainty as she pursued identifiable objectives in developing her relationship with the child.

In this kind of situation many different problems of transference could be identified. But the setting and structure permitted most of these problems to be resolved without too much difficulty. Thus, when a youngster attempted seduction of his teacher-mom by regression or calculated acts of provocation, simple identification for the teacher-mom of what was happening was frequently sufficient to permit her to handle the situation appropriately and with her own techniques. The teacher-mom thus felt much freer to experiment, since she became aware of the process of identification geared only to what was happening. She was not molded into a preconceived set of reactions and responses. This slowly stimulated a kind of integrity and purpose among the teacher-moms, and they developed a degree of professionalism that was impressive to see. As they worked side by side with their children and each other, there emerged a continual process of identification which could be heard at coffee-break time, group activity period, and other moments of the day. When one child presented a particularly difficult problem the teacher-moms would frequently focus on it, using their collective abilities to work it out, and when the need arose physically helping each other.

It is important to stress that this system of checks and counter-checks developed spontaneously out of the idea that

a one-to-one relationship was essential for the education and
training of these children. But once this process was identified
it was permitted to develop, not with the intent of developing
therapeutic relationships between the teacher-moms and the
children, but rather with the recognition of the contribution
it was making to meaningful communication. It set the stage
for the primary goal of stimulating the learning process and
thus making teaching possible.

The interaction between teacher-mom and child was not
always a constructive one. In some instances the children were
able to reconstruct successfully elements in the patterns of
their disturbed relationships. Once they accomplished this,
they seemed motivated to perpetuate them. When this
occurred, the teacher-mom might participate to the degree
that her own relationship with the child would become disturbed. In several instances this kind of process became
irreversible and it was found that the teacher-mom had become, unknowingly, motivated to perpetuate the very problem
that was interfering with the learning process.

In several such instances identification of the problem to
the teacher-mom was not enough. When this occurred it was
possible to change the teacher-mom to another child. This
was facilitated by the movement of children in and out of the
project. This gradual shifting of the project population permitted a climate which encouraged changes in relationship to
take place without the usual problems associated with such
disruption. It rarely disturbed the child since interrupting a
process of the type described would relieve him of the anxiety
attached to his own behavior. Decisions for such changes were
usually the result of careful examination of the dynamics and
discussion with all the people involved. There were enough
ancillary personnel involved with the child so that such a
change could never be viewed as a total break in relationship.

In many ways the project emerged as a kind of communal
matriarchal grouping where all the adults took on a teacher-

mom role. It became the accepted pattern, and once established new adults and new children could be introduced at will, since the core of the communal milieu was always present and self-perpetuating. In its own way this communal system became a most productive setting for tolerating disturbed behavior, initiating change, and developing new modes of interaction. It was protective to both child and teacher-mom by its very organization. Not only did it blend the essential ingredients for meaningful relationships, it also safeguarded the individuals involved so that new experience, change, disruption of old patterns, could take place without anxiety.

The more personal emotional reactions of the teacher-moms can be only partially identified. There must have been tremendous satisfaction for most of them. The majority have remained with the project over a number of years, and this kind of devotion can stem only from personal gains experienced. It was almost as if their own identity as women and mothers had become reinforced in this new, socially productive, community-oriented role. In many instances the women said the project was more gratifying than most of their other social and community activities. And this certainly is understandable. They were able to continue a well-established pattern of gratification in terms of their own fulfillment, and at the same time assume a prestige role of participation in one of the solid and accepted institutions of the community, the school system itself. Apparently most of the women responded with a sense of fulfillment. They gave up nothing, and by their participation were able to add to a well-established system from which all had obtained considerable satisfaction in the past. From the response and reactive patterns of the teacher-moms there was little doubt that their experience was rewarding. Whether we can identify the critical factors which made it so rewarding or not, the important point was their dramatic contribution to the project itself and their extraordinary contribution to the welfare of the children.

7 The Elmont Project and the Community

VISITORS to the Elmont project frequently ask what is being done for the parents and families of the children. When the project was first started, it was felt by the professional staff that some group meetings of the parents should be undertaken. This is in line with the thinking of many professionals dealing with seriously disturbed children. They feel that not much can be accomplished unless inroads are made simultaneously on the family pathology, since this so often exists as a contributing and sometimes aggravating circumstance. In fact, many professionals will refuse to try to help the child unless the parents are willing to participate in concomitant group or individual therapy.

Accordingly, the parents of the original six children in the Elmont project were invited by the school administrator to a meeting with the psychologists, the consulting psychiatrist, the head school physician, and himself. It should be remembered that all of these parents had met the psychologist and the psychiatrist previously one or more times. Some had met the school administrator and the head school physician. The meeting was a total and complete failure and a waste of everyone's time. It is possible the professionals were inept, but this is doubtful because all are unusually well-trained. The consulting psychiatrist—one of the co-authors—had been in charge of the children's wards at Bellevue Hospital. He was quite successful with this group technique as medical director of the League School for Emotionally Disturbed Children in Brooklyn, New York, and of the West Nassau Community Mental Health Center, as well as in his private practice. The fact of the matter is that this meeting served to confirm what all the professionals knew anyhow: that many of the parents had no real understanding of what was operative either in their child or in their own family relationships, and did not want to know. Or if they did know, they refused to face it.

As a result, no further meetings of a group nature were scheduled. The decision was taken that all contact with the parents would be accomplished by the professionals, particularly by the psychologist, the teacher-in-charge, or the school nurse-teacher in her social work capacity. In addition it was decided that under no circumstances would the parents be permitted to contact the teacher-moms or visit the project. The only time parents are allowed at the project is prior to the in-take of their child, if they wish to see the project in operation and if the professional staff feels it might be helpful for them to see it.

The Elmont educational administrator took this position with complete awareness that this policy was contrary to the established theory and practice of professionals working in the field. "Let's see what can be done with these children," he said in effect, "even if we don't get desirable cooperation and understanding from all of the parents." The results, to date, speak for themselves. It is not only possible but probable, even under adverse family circumstances, that seriously emotionally disturbed children can become healthier with the approach used by the Elmont public schools. It is further evident that gains made with the children seem to remain after the children are no longer in the project, but are still living in the family environments. It has been established, also, that as some of the children become healthier it seems to trigger changes for the better in some of the families.

Comments of some of the parents are particularly revealing. The father of Elliott indicates that Elliott is more controllable at home, although he continues to respond better to his father than to his grandmother. He fits into more situations, such as being able to sit through a movie or go shopping, without creating havoc. He seems to have become less aggressive in his actions toward other children. His father would like to see Elliott in more group activities, despite the fact that Elliott is not yet ready, which the father has never understood. When asked whether or not he ever considered placing Elliott in an institution he said he had. There is a school run by a county agency where, he says, he was told there were three types of classes: for trainable retardates, for brain-injured children of normal intelligence, and for emotionally disturbed children with no physical disabilities and of normal intelligence. Elliott could not, of course, fit into any of these groups.

A mother indicated that when the school district first told her her son was to be transferred to the special project she was against it, because "I heard it was for retarded children." She felt better about it, however, after the psychologist explained the purpose of the special project and its program and methods. She was most positive in her praise of the staff, both professional and volunteer. "Everyone is so nice, even the bus driver; they all made him feel special." (Ludwig Scaglione, who drives the station-wagon that transports the children to and from the special project, is one of the project's best "psychologists." He has a happy, cheerful, outgoing disposition and enormous common sense in dealing with the children.)

This mother said her son loved his teacher-moms and talked a great deal about them at home. Both she and her husband were very satisfied with what the project has accomplished, since her son's behavior "has definitely improved at home." After her son had been at the project for several months she said he began commenting at home that he was "sorry" for some of the other children. "He used to make fun of everybody before and now he doesn't. I am glad I went along with it. Ever since, I've been like a psychologist myself." Contacted after her son was placed in a regular classroom, she said the staff "gave wonderful help. They told me to call any time I had questions and I did a few times, and they were very helpful." She said her son was now doing pretty well in the regular classroom, except "once in a while he daydreams." She said he likes his present teacher and has made more friends than he ever could before. He also gets along much better with his brother. His teacher, interestingly enough at this point, reported that he was doing average work and that she had no complaints about his behavior.

The mother did not mention to relatives or friends that her son was in the special project until he had been there for some time. When she did tell them about it, they all were favorably disposed to the idea and indicated that they could see improvement in his behavior. She did not discuss it with any of the neighbors until one of them asked her why her son was being picked up by the school bus. After she told her something about the special project and why her son was in it, this neighbor, who formerly was critical of her son, said she would try to help. The mother reported that the woman did become less severe. She felt that this type of special project is the responsibility of the school, and would recommend that other school districts start similar projects: "As long as they know how to talk to the mother about it and don't just send home a piece of paper." She also felt that parents should be warned not to "ask other people's advice who don't know anything about it. They tell you all sorts of things that aren't true." One person told her that if her son were placed in the project this would "be a black mark which will be with him all his life"; and that people could "check his records and this would go against him." Another person told her it was not a good thing to do because even if a child were "not like them, he will soon start acting like them." She later found out, first from the psychologist and later from her own experience, that none of these observations was true.

She feels the government should help schools and communities to provide needed special programs. She also feels, however, "that everyone should help in some way. They could donate funds or volunteer help." She had never contacted any other agency for help regarding her son and never considered placing him in an institution. In general, she feels that children should not be placed in institutions: "They wouldn't get the individual attention like my son did. You get faster results if you work with one at a time."

She reported that she has become more aware of community mental health problems and is more responsive to fund drives than before. She has become more understanding of the problems and needs of the troubled child. "You hear about it, but it never really hits home unless you know of someone, or it hits you."

Another mother said she was very happy when the school suggested that her daughter be placed in the special project. "It was wonderful for her. She loved it at the special project and liked everyone there and everyone liked her. She's very affectionate." Relatives, friends, and neighbors all "thought it was a wonderful thing."

She had contacted other agencies prior to her daughter's reaching school age: "When I found out about my daughter, I didn't know what I was going to do. I took her to a local hospital facility for an examination. They said they couldn't help. I thought of taking her to the 'C.P.' Center, but she didn't really need this. Then I went to a 'C.P.' specialist in New York City and he said I should take her to the 'C.P.' Clinic for Physical Therapy and Speech. Her speech has improved a lot."

This mother feels she is more aware of mental health problems in the community now than she was before contact with the special project. She is more responsive to the fund drives now. "Once you are in it yourself, you feel like helping all you can." She feels that projects like the Elmont special project are something the schools should do, and that "The state and everybody should help all they can." She never considered placing her daughter in an institution and would not advocate doing so with any children.

A foster-mother stated that when the psychologist first suggested placing her foster-son in the special project two years ago, she was very pleased. He had not been able to get along in a group at all and had become very difficult to cope with, and she was afraid the agency was going to take the child from her and place him in an institution.

This is her foster-son's second year in the special project and she states he is very happy there. "He loves his teacher-moms and talks about them a lot and he's crazy about the bus driver." She reports that he is also "very fond" of the staff members, and pointed out that when he was sick they wrote to him, called on the phone and visited him, which made him very happy. She reported that there has been a great change in his behavior since his attendance at the special project. He is "more grown-up now, both at home and when he is play-ing." She feels that he is much more able to play with other children than he was before, and as a result he now has more friends. He is reading very well now, which she finds rather surprising. She feels that his academic progress is directly attributable to the fact that he works alone with his teacher and is "not made nervous" or distracted by other children.

She stated that as a result of the child's relationship with the special project and her talks with the staff members, she has gained more understanding of the brain-injured or emo-tionally disturbed child. Furthermore, she has become more aware of community mental health problems in general and more responsive to mental health fund drives. Friends and relatives to whom she has talked about the special project have had favorable reactions to the idea, and have noticed improvement in her foster-son's behavior. She feels that this kind of project is the responsibility of the school and that the state should give financial aid to communities to help them initiate and maintain such projects. "I often sit and think what would have happened to my foster-son and us if the program had not been there. . . . All I want is for him to be able to grow up and hold a job. I hope they keep the project going." She had never considered institutionalizing him as a solution to his problem, but feared that he might have had to be if his behavior had not improved. Asked if she had contacted any other agency for help, she stated that she had looked into a private nursery school that someone had recom-mended, but found it beyond their financial resources.

Another mother said that when the school first suggested her son be placed in the special project she was worried about what was going to become of him. Now she feels that the special project has helped him in some ways, but it seems to be "bringing out the baby in him. He wants a lot of my attention. He will help around the house and work if I give him money for it. He gives up very easily on almost anything. I had another son like this one but the principal of the school bent over backwards to help him. He still doesn't read very well." She stated that her son likes going to the special project and he likes his teacher-moms. She personally has no particular feelings about them one way or the other. She stated that his behavior at home has improved some but he still argues with his sister a great deal. "He likes to cook and he fixes his own lunch. He also shows me his homework." When asked if he has more friends now than formerly, she reported that "He never really had very many and he could always take them or leave them. He does have one friend that he goes to visit." At this point she went on to explain that from the time he was three years old he has always wandered away from home, but he has always somehow managed to find his way back.

When asked if her contact with the special project and its staff had made her any more aware of community mental health problems she replied, "I watch for special programs on television. I watch them and I try to get my son to watch them, too."

The family has only one other relative living in the area and, although he is aware that her son is in the special project, he has expressed no opinion concerning this. She has never discussed it with any of her friends or neighbors.

When asked if she felt the government should help communities to establish special projects such as the Elmont project she replied, "I don't know. It's something new to me. If my son really needs help, maybe he should be in a clinic. I do worry about him. But what with working, I can't get away all the time to keep track of him."

She went on to explain that he was very upset last summer because he could not go away. She went to her religious charity organization to see if he could go to their sleep-away camp, but they would not accept him. Her parting words about her son were, "He is lazy and he doesn't like to work or read. He didn't even like to be read to when he was younger." The one change to the good that she could report was that he is now sending away for things he sees in magazines.

The mother of a little girl said that when the school first suggested her daughter be placed in the special project, she thought it would be a wonderful idea because she would get more special attention. She reported that the special project "did wonders for my daughter. She learned to understand her handicap and this helped her to overcome frustration. She came a long way in her school work and understood it more."

Relatives and neighbors with whom the mother discussed the Elmont special project felt that it was a good idea, and would probably be very helpful to her daughter, because "A regular school cannot devote full time to individual attention." But some of her relatives wondered if, after having this individual attention, she might not find it difficult to return to regular classes. The daughter was very fond of her teacher-moms and, although she is no longer at the special project, still remembers them. She is now back in regular school and doing second grade work. She has learned how to get along better with her friends, both at school and at home.

The mother feels that this type of program is a responsibility of the school and she feels that in every community there must be people who "could get together and form such a thing." She feels the state government should provide financial assistance to such projects.

When asked if she had contacted other agencies for help, she replied that she had gone to a children's rehabilitation center and a special school. She had never considered placing her daughter in an institution, and, in general, feels no child should be institutionalized until he has been given "a fair chance by the family and the public in general."

She stated that she has become more aware of community mental health problems and more responsive to their fund drives.

Steve's mother said that when the school first suggested he be placed in the special project she thought it was a very good idea. "I had watched him in a regular class and he couldn't take it." She feels that his experience in the special project has been "marvelous for him. He is not as upset as he was and this is wonderful to see, but I worry about what will happen to him when he is older and will have to leave the program. I have wondered a little if there was something else that might help him more. With Steve, the learning end of it doesn't matter so much—he learns on his own. From what I've been told, he needs to get help in learning to live with others."

She reported that Steve has liked all of his teacher-moms and she herself thinks it is wonderful of these women to give their time to help. Steve also likes the staff members and she has found them to be most understanding and helpful. His behavior at home has improved to some extent, in that he can play better with his sister now. However, certain aspects of his behavior have not changed much. He still "gets to quite a high point of frustration around the end of October and stays there until the end of February, when he begins to improve again. Also, his moods and behavior still swing from one extreme to the other, and he still gets very upset on his birthday and at Christmas. Steve tries to do what he should, but somehow he can't. He will dress himself now." She feels that one of Steve's problems is his father, in whom Steve "can see nothing that he would want to copy. I suppose parents sometimes even give up. But Steve has acted very different to me than to anyone else. The kindergarten teacher couldn't stand him and he knew this so he wouldn't speak. He couldn't stand to have anyone touch him except me. Lately, it seems even an object—when he touches an object by accident, he must reach out and touch it. He is still concerned about getting revenge."

They have recently moved into a neighborhood "where parents don't want children around and some of them know Steve from before." In general, the children are a little afraid of him, although the boy next door occasionally comes to play. From time to time she has wondered if perhaps Steve would get better faster if he were placed in an institution, but she would "certainly hate to have to do it. His attachment to me is very strong and it would be very hard for him, but it would be good for him to get away from his father."

Her relatives have never expressed any opinion about the Elmont project, but have told her that Steve seems to have improved. None of her friends have expressed opinions concerning the project either, but "People who have known him see that he is happier now and not as withdrawn."

When asked if she had contacted other agencies for help, she reported that some years ago she had taken Steve to a doctor who suggested group therapy. Following that she took him to a state clinic to be examined. Then, a neighbor suggested that she talk to a rabbi who sent her to a psychiatrist. This psychiatrist was also the psychiatrist for the school district and he referred Steve to the special project.

She feels that the kind of program offered by the special project should be provided by the school and that the state government should help by establishing standards and providing additional funds to the schools.

She stated that since her contact with the special project and its staff, she has really thought about community mental health problems for the first time and is more responsive to mental health fund drives.

She reported that she has been attending, when she feels well enough, group counseling sessions at the local mental health clinic. Her husband usually refuses to attend, however,

which annoys her because she feels that he is the one really
needing the help.

When the school first suggested that her son be placed in
the special project, one mother "felt bad, sort of ashamed. I
wondered what the neighbors would think. Now, the neighbors don't matter; they can't do anything for him and the
special project can." She reports that her son likes attending
the special project and he likes the staff and the teacher-
moms. "They seem to do the right thing at the right time."
She herself has no opinions concerning the teacher-moms, but
she does feel that the psychologists on the staff "hold back;
they don't give advice."

Since his attendance at the special project, her son's behavior has improved some. "Now, when he is at his best, he
can read and do things." The mother reported that he adjusts
well now to the neighbors. He is not so excitable or aggressive,
and he wants to please. None of her relatives think there is
anything wrong with him, so she has not discussed with them
his being in the special project. One of her neighbors reacted
badly when she first heard about it. "She said that he was
sick and that he was liable to hurt other children."

She is not sure whose responsibility it is, but she is sure
that communities should provide the type of program and
service that the special project provides. "There seem to be
so many of this sort of child. We need special schools. It's
actually dangerous to have this kind of child at home without
help." She stated that she had never approached any other
agency for help and had never considered placing him in an
institution. "That would be a criminal thing." She reported
that since her contact with the special project she has become
more aware of community mental health problems and is
more receptive to mental health fund drives, because "I feel
badly for those that can't be helped." She reported that she
had been going to the local mental health clinic for family

counseling, but quit recently because she could no longer afford it.

While these parents' comments were generally favorable, it would be an error to leave the impression that all parents feel this way. One who did not was the mother of a little boy. When interviewed she spent much time persuading the interviewer to intervene in her behalf with the project staff. She spent most of the time explaining her philosophy of child rearing, which is largely one of "children should be seen but not heard," and severe punishment for the smallest misbehavior or forgetfulness. She pointed out, also, that she is a very particular housekeeper. She spent additional time complaining that, in essence, the school district has given her a hard time because of her son. She frequently interrupted her discourse to ask the interviewer, "Don't you think I'm right?" or "Don't you agree that's the way it should be?"

When the school psychologist first suggested that her son be placed in the special project she thought it might be a good idea because "he would get special attention." Now she is beginning to change her mind. This past year he has been attending the project along with regular classes on a part-time basis. She feels that the special project has not been too good for him because, she thinks, "Maybe he picks up the bad behavior of the other kids there." Also, he complains to her that he would rather go to regular school full-time and not go to the special project at all. She feels that it might be better to let him try. "Maybe one of the reasons he doesn't behave too good is that he has too many teachers to adjust to."

She reported that his behavior at home is about the same as it was before he entered the special project. He does play better with younger children than he used to. However, he still has no friends. "There aren't many children his age in the neighborhood." She had no feelings one way or the other about the teacher-moms; she guessed, "They are all right."

However, she expressed rather negative feelings about the project professional staff and other school personnel in general. She seemed to feel they just don't understand her point of view or how difficult her home situation is, because the stepfather "doesn't like the boy." They also do not seem to understand the necessity for her punishing him so frequently, "But if I don't, how else is he going to learn?" From her point of view, the son is a very difficult child to live with because he does not mind well, and no matter how often or severely he is punished there are some things he just won't learn. Furthermore, on those occasions when a child has come into the house to play with him, they have made such a mess that she has had to send the child home, punish her son for his misbehavior, and then spend an hour or two getting the house back into "apple pie order."

At this point, she went on to describe an incident that had happened a few days before. The boy was brought home from the project one morning for misbehaving, an event which she found personally humiliating. "I just can't understand why he won't learn that when he behaves like that it embarrasses me. He was so upset at being sent home that he vomited all over the floor in the hall, in his room, and in the bathroom. The school psychologist told me not to punish him, but my mother would never have let me get away with that kind of behavior when I was a kid. If I had been sent home from school, she would have given me a good beating."

Her relatives are aware that her son is in the special project, but have expressed no opinions concerning it except to point out that as far as they can see he doesn't behave much better than he did before. She has not discussed her son or the project with any of her friends or neighbors. She guesses that the school should provide special projects. "It's good for some children." She does not think that the state government should give financial or any other kind of assistance to communities for this type of project: "They are already doing enough." She is no more aware of community mental health needs than she was before and she still does not contribute to mental health fund drives. "I've never paid much attention to it."

While most parents are generally pleased with what is being accomplished and are grateful, some have no appreciation or awareness of the unusual effort being expended on behalf of their children. Nonetheless the children continue to progress, and that is the purpose of the special project. In this connection it is interesting to observe the impact of what little publicity the program has received. Each time anything has appeared in print for the lay public, the Elmont district has received a considerable volume of mail and telephone calls from parents, asking if the special project could admit their child who has the same kind of impairment as the special project children. This, of course, is not possible, since Elmont School District 16 is a public school district, and can accommodate only children of people living within the district. There have been two instances where parents have sold their houses and relocated in Elmont to make their children eligible. The mail and telephone calls emphasize the desperation of parents seeking help, and the need for communities all over the country to provide it.

One of the concerns expressed at every professional meeting is how the professional staff of the Elmont school district feels about the special project, with its utilization of non-professional volunteers. This is what some of the professionals in the district say:

The supervising principal of the district, Dr. Ray L. Lindbloom, observes that the prevailing philosophy of the district has been, for many years, a solid belief that the public schools have a responsibility to educate all the educable children of all of the people of the district. He states that the idea for the special project was "evolved as the assistant for instruction and pupil personnel services [one of the co-authors] tried to relate pupil personnel services to the total educational needs of the district." It was found that some children could not be handled in the classrooms of the district. Therefore, the district became committed to the idea of identifying individual and gross needs of children, and adapting to them. The special project is a logical adaptation to the needs of this special group, like any other kind of special schedule that might be arranged as part of the regular program in one of the district's buildings; or like paying tuition and transportation for a paraplegic child to the adaptive program of "Abilities, Inc."

The supervising principal feels the special project has done a job for these youngsters beyond all expectations. It has proved that there is a practical way to meet the needs of these children who would normally be excluded. He thinks the special project stems from the basic philosophy of the school district. He feels that personnel who have had contact with the special project staff or children have more understanding of the behavior not only of the schizophrenic and brain-injured child, but of other behavior-problem children as well. He says that all school personnel are now more conscious of the subject of mental health and tend to incorporate more information concerning it in their teaching. In his opinion the special project is one of a number of forces responsible for increased awareness.

Insofar as the role of government is concerned, he thinks that state aid should be available but should be controlled at the county level. He feels that the state could provide a very real service by establishing a coordinating agency, perhaps an *ad hoc* committee with a paid administrator.

The supervising principal considers the special project a great success, not only in terms of the help it has given individual children but also in terms of improved morale of the classroom teacher. "She now knows that there is professional help available to assist her in working with and keeping the child in a classroom as long as possible, and feels a sense of relief in knowing that, when the child can no longer be maintained in the classroom, there is some place for him to go." He would not hesitate to recommend this approach to other school districts as long as they are aware of the spadework that must be done to gain the support of the school board and the community. In his opinion these children would not benefit more by being placed in an institution: "The beauty of this arrangement is that he can maintain a fairly normal life."

He volunteered that the results of the special project do have implications concerning the establishment of educational and treatment programs for junior high and high school youngsters who are emotionally disturbed. He pointed out that the one-to-one relationship which this type of program offers is needed by many: "At least it means that we can think about something other than institutional care."

Of the three school board members asked to comment, two first heard about the special project at its inception and the third heard about it a year and a half ago, when he joined the school board. The initial reaction of all three was that it was an excellent idea and would provide a much needed service. They remain enthusiastic and feel it has been a great success. They all offered that, although the project has received very little publicity, it has been well received in the community and has always had total support from the school board.

When asked if they feel this type of project is a responsibility of the school district, two stated that in their opinion it is not. The board president feels that some separate agency is needed, with sufficient staff to train people working closely with the mental health clinic and educators. The other person stated, "Those that are not educable come more under welfare." However, they both agree that since no one else was doing the job in Elmont, the school district had to attempt to do it to the best of its ability. A third member believes that it is a responsibility of the school district, but that the community needs much more state aid.

Concerning the use of volunteers, they had mixed feelings. One said: "Any project that has to depend on volunteers has a basic weakness, but at least it is a step in the right direction." A second felt that lay people should not attempt to teach and that these children should have teachers with special training. The third said the use of the volunteer is not only good but essential, for without them the special project would "be outrageously expensive."

It was the feeling of all that knowledge of the progress of the children in the special project has made the school board more aware of some of the needs of these children. All agreed that the assistant to the supervising principal had been largely responsible for getting the special project started and keeping it going. Said one: "We need one of him in every community." All three think that more federal and state subsidization should be provided for special educational programs. One pointed out that long-range planning is difficult when a project such as this is paid for by many organizations, voluntary and governmental, "throwing money in the pot."

They all agreed that, in their opinion, these children would not benefit more by being placed in institutions. One of them stated, "One of the prime reasons for this project is to help the children get back into school with other children. It is a transitional approach which an institution cannot offer."

All seven of the school principals interviewed first heard about the special project at its inception, and all thought, at the time, that it seemed like an excellent idea. All but one now feel even more enthusiastic than they did at the beginning. The one exception still approves but has begun to wonder if perhaps too much time is being spent with too few children. He feels that other children with similar though less severe problems are not now getting the attention they should. There were various responses to a question regarding misgivings about the program. Four principals had no particular misgivings; one indicated that too much time was being devoted to too few children; another was concerned that it provided assistance only to the grade school child; and the seventh mentioned two points: (1) that the project should include some less seriously disturbed children, and (2) that the use of volunteers can be dangerous if they are allowed to make a professional's decisions. (This, of course, is not permitted.)

When asked what they felt was particularly good about the special project, six mentioned the one-to-one relationship and the seventh said the fact that the project has been a success. Some other points made by the principals were: (1) the special project helps children who otherwise would not have an education, (2) it has value to the teacher-moms, (3) there is no loss of teacher-pupil relationship.

When asked which one person or group of persons they felt was primarily responsible for initiating and carrying out the special project, all seven agreed that the assistant to the supervising principal undoubtedly acted as the primary spark. Two of them felt that additional necessary support came from the school psychiatrist and psychologists. One felt that the interest of all the personnel in the school district, along with the interest of the parents, gave added support. A third felt that the interest of the rabbi at the Jewish Center had helped to sustain it.

Four of the principals offered, without reservation, that this type of project is the responsibility of the school. Two agreed, provided that it does not cause a deficit in other areas. Another agreed, provided that education, not therapy, is the goal. The seventh principal felt that it is not the responsibility of the public schools, because the schools should be geared to the normal child and there should be separate schools with special educators for the deviant. All seven agreed that they would recommend the concept of the special project to other school districts and communities, but four mentioned these reservations: (1) too much time should not be given to too few children; (2) the volunteers must be carefully selected; (3) someone was needed like the assistant to the supervising principal in Elmont to get the project set in motion.

They all agreed that they have gained more understanding of the behavior of the schizophrenic and brain-injured child and that their understanding of other behavior-problem children has been reinforced by the special project. Five of the seven offered that the understanding gained has helped them to work more effectively with these children and their parents. Two feel that, because of their own previous experience, the special project has not added appreciably to their ability to work with the children or their parents. They all indicated that it has helped the teachers who have had contact with a child before or after he was placed in the special project.

Their opinions were divided as to whether or not the special project has been responsible for the addition of other adaptive procedures in the schools. Four felt that it probably has; two said that the special project itself is actually the result of the total guidance program; one had no opinion.

They all agreed that they are now more alert to the mental health needs of the community at large and most of them give more support to mental health fund drives. However, they indicated this interest and support was not necessarily a result of the special project. They stated that the majority of teachers in the district are more aware of mental health needs and include more information concerning mental health in their curriculum content. But again they agreed that this increase in interest and use of material is due to a number of factors in addition to the influence of the special project.

They all agreed that there has been greater emphasis given to the inclusion of mental health information in the in-service training program, but feel that this is due to a combination of factors—including the pupil-personnel services program, the increased publicity given to mental health in all mass media, and, to some extent, the special project itself. In general, they all said there should be more state aid given for projects of this kind. One principal felt that state aid should be given, provided control of the money was left to the local community or school district.

It was the opinion of all the principals that, in general, these children would not benefit more from being placed in an institution than from participating in the special project. Three indicated there might be instances in which the home situation was so detrimental that the child might respond better if removed from the home and placed in an institution.

They all agreed that the results of the special project have implications for the treatment of troubled junior high and high school youngsters. Two questioned whether youngsters of high school age could benefit, but agreed that the project should be expanded to include junior high school children.

The six school nurse-teachers revealed that their initial reaction upon hearing about the project was that it was a good idea. They all are now very enthusiastic about it because so many of the children have been returned to the classroom. They all believe it has been responsible, directly or indirectly, for the adoption of other adaptive procedures to meet the children's needs. They pointed to the use of supplementary teachers and of special teachers for children needing individual attention, to staffing conferences, and to the fact that teachers have become more aware and more willing to talk about children with problems.

They all agree that this type of project is the responsibility of the school and they all would recommend to other communities that such projects be initiated.

It was the opinion of all six that the assistant to the super-

vising principal was primarily responsible for the initiation
and development of the special project. Two mentioned that
its continued success was due also to the support and cooperation of the psychologists, the rabbi, and the volunteers.

All felt that the special project and staffing conferences
have helped them to gain more understanding of the behavior
of schizophrenic or brain-injured children and of other behavior-problem children. It has also become possible for them
to work more effectively with such children and their parents.
The existence of the special project has helped the nurse-
teachers give reassurance and support to the parent who
wonders, when it becomes apparent that his child cannot cope
with the classroom, what is to become of his child.

They all agreed that, although the special project had not
made them any more aware of community mental health
needs, it had reinforced their previously held beliefs that such
problems exist. It made them feel more hopeful that something could be done to alleviate them. They agreed that classroom teachers have been making increasing use of the school
nurse-teacher as a resource person in two ways: (1) to discuss
with them some of the "problem" children in their classes;
(2) to request additional materials concerning mental health
that they might use in the classroom. The nurse-teachers
thought this may have resulted from a combination of factors,
including increased public interest in mental health, staffing
conferences, the guidance program, and the special project.

When asked what particular misgivings they had about the
special project, three had none. Two said these children
should have specially trained teachers rather than volunteers
working with them, and one of these two was concerned because the Jewish Center's nursery school is in the same building. She also indicated that the special project needs to do
more about developing an intensive therapy program for the
parents. The sixth nurse-teacher felt there had not been
enough communication with the school personnel concerning

the special project. She said, too, that the special project should be housed in one of the school buildings.

When asked what they thought was particularly good about the special project, four mentioned the one-to-one relationship. The remaining two mentioned the fact that the child is able to remain in his own community and family. It was the opinion of all that the majority of these children would not benefit more by being placed in an institution than they have, or can, from the special project. They agreed that every attempt must be made to work with the child in the community so that he can remain in as familiar and normal an environment as possible. They did indicate that there may be instances when the home situation is so damaging and uncooperative that the child might be better able to respond in an institutional setting. The nurse-teachers all thought the state should give additional financial aid.

All agreed that the success of the special project has implications for the development of similar programs for youngsters of junior high and high school age. They felt that it should be expanded to include youngsters who have somewhat less severe problems but who are disruptive and difficult to control and who get little benefit from the classroom setting.

A school psychologist who was not involved at the beginning of the special project stated that she thought it was an excellent idea when it was first proposed and that she continues to think so. She has had no particular misgivings about the special project. In her opinion the two most outstanding things about the special project are: (1) it provides the child with a one-to-one relationship; and (2) it allows him to gain acceptance and success and still continue his academic work so that he can be returned to the classroom.

In her opinion, the assistant to the supervising principal was largely responsible for initiating and carrying out the project. She definitely thinks that the type of project offered is a responsibility of the school, and she would certainly recommend to other communities that they initiate similar projects.

She stated that the special project has resulted, to some extent, in other adaptive procedures in the schools to meet the needs of individual children. She pointed out that there has been less resistance on the part of school personnel to establishing such procedures and that there is now much less tendency to try to use the special project as a dumping ground for children who are behavior problems in the classroom. She feels that the school administrators and, to some extent, teachers, are more aware of the mental health needs of the community, but this awareness cannot necessarily be attributed to the special project alone. She suggested that the special project was partially responsible for (1) the development of staffing conferences, and (2) the setting up of faculty meetings at which a psychologist or some other specialist from the pupil personnel services talked and worked with the teachers.

In her opinion, the children served by the special project would not benefit more by being placed in an institution, except in those instances where the family is abnormally negative and uncooperative. In those instances it is possible that the child might respond better if he were removed from the home and placed in an institution.

She believes that the state should provide additional funds to school districts for emotionally disturbed children. She thought that the success of the special project does have implications for the development of educational and treatment programs for troubled youngsters in other age groups. The younger children, however, would probably benefit more from this particular type of project.

The initial reactions of eleven classroom teachers were positive. They thought it was a good idea when they first heard about it, and continue to think so. Five of these teachers have had contact with children from the special project and have had an opportunity to work with the psychologists. Two of the others have visited the special project and talked with the staff there. All seven agree it has helped them to a better understanding of the needs of these children and of behavior-problem children in general. They also think it has helped them to work more effectively with the children and their parents. The remaining four feel they have derived little help or benefit from the special project.

All eleven agree that staffing conferences and opportunities to meet with the psychologists and psychiatrist have been particularly helpful in gaining knowledge and understanding of disturbed and brain-injured children and in learning how to work most effectively with them. They agreed that the type of program provided by the special project is the responsibility of the school as long as it does not detract from the evaluation and guidance services needed by all the children. All eleven indicated they would recommend the establishment of similar projects in other communities and school districts.

When asked if they had any misgivings about the special project, nine stated they had none in particular. Two questioned whether the volunteers were sufficiently qualified and wondered what sort of training they received. They thought the most outstandingly good things about the special project were: the establishment of one-to-one relationship; the observable progress of the children involved; the love and attention given to the children, not only by the volunteers but by the professional staff; and the fact that it has afforded the classroom teacher the opportunity to work "hand-in-hand" with the psychologist.

They all expressed the opinion that the children would not have benefited more by being placed in an institution. They felt that every effort should be made to keep the children at home, and to work with them in as normal a setting as possible.

Seven were of the opinion that the assistant to the supervising principal was largely responsible for initiating the special project, and that he along with the psychologists, the curriculum specialist, and the volunteers were responsible for carrying it out. The remaining four were not sure who was responsible, but had assumed that it was the school administration. They all expressed the opinion that classroom teachers should be told more about the special project than to date they have been. Only one teacher stated that in her school the project had been discussed in a formal way at a staff meeting.

Teachers from the other six schools in the district stated that to their knowledge no such discussion had taken place and that any knowledge the teachers had of the special project had come from informal discussions with the school psychologist, discussions among themselves, or attendance at a staffing conference.

All agreed that, although they and other teachers are now more aware of community mental health problems and needs, the increase in awareness cannot be attributed to the special project alone. They felt it was partly the result of the special project, along with the pupil personnel services program, staffing conferences, and the fact that there has been a great increase in emphasis on mental health in the professional literature and in the mass media. They indicated that this combination was the reason for the increased use of mental health materials in curriculum content and in the in-service training program.

All agreed that the state government had a responsibility to help communities finance such special projects. Two of them said that it should also do something about establishing standards for such projects. One teacher thought the state and federal governments should supply scholarships and other incentives to encourage people to enter the fields of special education, guidance, psychology, etc. All agreed the success of the special project has real implications for community planning in the development of programs for children in other age groups.

The head school physician revealed that his initial reaction to the special project was that it had merit and would provide a very needed service for the school and the community. He is now very gratified at the way it has turned out and feels it has been a great step forward in the management of these children. It has inspired him to gain more knowledge and he is presently studying psychiatry and serving a residency in a child psychiatric clinic. He found that working with the project staff and children helped him to become more aware of family and other environmental problems that surround the physically ill child.

He said that this type of project is very definitely the responsibility of the school district: "The purpose of education is to prepare people for adult life. If the child cannot be educated by ordinary methods, it is the school's responsibility to find whatever method is necessary to provide the child with an education." He thought the government should assist the community to provide any special education services that are needed—not only financially, but also by providing consultation services and making research teams available.

The only misgiving he has concerning the special project is that it is housed in a non-school building. He is strongly in favor of using the volunteer teacher-moms because he feels they are more likely to accept the child as he is: "Perhaps it is a good thing that they don't have a professional background." He went on to point out that the project provides the volunteer with an opportunity to derive satisfaction from having offered herself. He stated that the most outstanding thing about the special project is the fact that these children would otherwise be excluded from school, education, and preparation for life, and would probably end in an institution: "The special project, in essence, is doing a real salvage job." In his opinion, the assistant to the supervising principal was primarily responsible for initiating the special project, and without him it would never "have gotten off the ground or been perpetuated." In his opinion, these children would definitely not benefit more by being placed in an institution. "No matter how bad a home is, the child will do better in his home setting."

The rabbi of the center where the special project is presently housed first heard about the project when he was approached by the assistant to the supervising principal, who asked if the center would be able to lend the use of its facilities. The project sounded interesting and valuable to him and he has become one of its most enthusiastic supporters. The supervisor of the nursery school and the secretary of the center were both told about the special project by the rabbi before it actually began. It sounded to them like a "wonderful thing." They still have very positive feelings about it. They all agree that the project does not interfere, to any great extent, with the routine at the center and they feel that it has been a great success. The rabbi stated that although no formal mention of the project has ever been made in the bulletin or any of the meetings of the temple or center the congregation is aware, pleased, and proud that their center has had a part in its development.

They all agree that these children would not benefit more by being placed in an institution, unless the home environment becomes so damaging that work at school is totally counteracted. The rabbi pointed out that many of these children have an organic basis for their disturbed behavior, and removing them from home reveals a pessimistic attitude in the parents that they can't be helped.

The nursery school supervisor and the center secretary said

that as a result of being in proximity to the special project they have become more aware of community mental health needs and give more support to the fund drives. Both thought that this kind of project probably is the responsibility of the school but that government should help communities to finance such programs. The rabbi stated that he is not sure whether it really is the legal responsibility of the school, but feels it is good that the school district did assume it. He agreed that the state should give the community monetary assistance, but only in terms of helping to evaluate programs and finance model projects. It should not be expected to finance such projects continuously. They all agreed that the success of this project has implications for the development of programs for youngsters of junior high and high school age. The rabbi stated that one implication is that the child has to be worked with at his own level.

Five members of the Kiwanis Club of Elmont were contacted. This organization has helped to finance the special project since its inception. All five first heard about the project when the assistant to the supervising principal approached the club for help. They reported that the idea was received enthusiastically by the entire club and that they are still enthusiastic and very pleased and proud they were able to assist. Three of the men have no misgivings about the special project. One, whose wife is a teacher-mom, complained the questionnaire the volunteers had to complete was too technical and difficult; the fifth was worried about what might happen if the volunteers and the temple facilities were suddenly not available.

In their opinion, the most outstanding aspects of the program are: (1) the fact that a number of the children have already been returned to the classroom; (2) the opportunity for a one-to-one relationship; (3) the loyalty of, and the excellent work done by, the volunteers. All agree that a project such as this is the responsibility of the school and they would all recommend that other communities and school districts initiate similar projects. In their opinion, the assistant to the supervising principal was primarily responsible for initiating and carrying out the project, and they feel that its continued success is due to the support of the psychologists, the curriculum specialist, the rabbi, and the volunteers.

All five agree that the type of child served by the special project would not benefit more by being placed in an institution. All indicated that, in general, they thought no child should be placed in an institution except as a last resort. Three of the men indicated that, as a result of their support of this project, they have become more aware of, and interested in, the mental health needs of the community at large. They now give greater support to mental health fund drives. The other two have been active in the local mental health association for some time. They are all of the opinion that the state and county governments should provide financial assistance to initiate and maintain this type of project.

When asked why the Kiwanis Club chose to support this program, they pointed out that Kiwanis is specifically interested in helping the underprivileged child. This project appeared to be a unique opportunity to provide a much needed service to a group of children no one else wanted to help. They stated that many other chapters of Kiwanis throughout the nation have been extremely interested, and some have indicated they would be interested in similar programs in their own communities. Both the national and state magazines have published articles concerning the special project.

They stated that relatives, friends, and co-workers to whom they have mentioned it have all reacted positively and wished to learn more about it. They all feel that since the project has been so successful, the community should begin to think in terms of expanding it or initiating some other similar project to meet the needs of troubled youngsters of other age groups.

To find out how a professional in the mental health field felt about the special project, the administrative director of the community mental health center, which serves Elmont and some neighboring communities, was contacted.

He had heard about the special project during its planning phase. Initially, he had mixed feelings. He felt that anything that could be done would be good, but he wondered about the use of non-professionals to assist the teacher-in-charge. Now that the project has been successful he still has some, although fewer, migivings about the teacher-moms. Aside from questioning the use of volunteers however, he has no further misgivings. He feels that three of the outstanding features of the project are: (1) it has made use of available community resources—the Kiwanis Club, the Jewish Center, people with time available; (2) it has provided a one-to-one relationship for the child; and (3) it has permitted the child to be maintained in a school setting. These children would otherwise be "forced to spend the whole day with their mothers, who are often partially responsible for the disturbance."

He suggested that the special project has provided an understanding of the way that education can work, and has given the community an additional resource. It has pointed out the importance of the one-to-one relationship in teaching, and this has implications in working with youngsters in other age groups. In his opinion, the assistant to the supervising principal was largely responsible for initiating and carrying out the special project. He believes this type of project is the responsibility of the school, and based upon the experiments in Elmont he would recommend to other communities and school districts that they initiate similar projects. He believes that the state should have a special program for the education of emotionally disturbed children and, because of the unusual expense involved in working with them, it should provide additional funds to school districts for this purpose.

In his opinion, the children involved in the special project would not benefit more from being placed in an institution. "They can exist in a community setting. Institutionalization is contra-indicated and should be used only as a last resort." He indicated that the attitudes of the general public are definitely moving in the direction of greater acceptance of maintaining and treating the emotionally disturbed and mentally ill in the community.

He sees the role of the mental health clinic, in relation to the school, as one of providing consultation, diagnosis, and treatment where indicated, and of functioning in liaison for counseling parents whose children have been placed in the project.

Contacts were made with some of the religious leaders in the community, including the rabbi of the reformed temple, the minister of a Protestant church, and a monsignor, the pastor of one of the Catholic parishes. The minister heard about the special project at the Kiwanis meeting when the assistant to the supervising principal made his appeal for funds. The rabbi first heard about it when he arrived in Elmont three years ago, and the monsignor first heard about it a year or so ago. They all had favorable reactions to the idea and have still. They agreed it has proved itself a valuable adjunct to the regular school program. In fact, the minister feels it should be expanded and publicized, "with due decorum." He would recommend that other communities initiate similar projects, but neither the rabbi nor the monsignor feel they know enough about the special project to make such a recommendation. Both the minister and the monsignor feel that such a project is a responsibility of the school. They all believe the state should provide additional funds to help finance such projects, and should also, along with the federal government, do something to facilitate the recruitment and training of competent personnel. The monsignor pointed out that new legislation would be needed to obtain additional funds for school districts.

The minister felt that the children served by the special project would not benefit more by being placed in an institution. "I don't think they would have comparable attention, nor the same personal touch." The rabbi indicated that he was not qualified to judge. In his opinion, however, if a child can function in society at all he should remain there. The monsignor felt that he knew so little about the special project or the children it serves that he was in no position to answer the question.

All agreed that aside from the women who are both volunteers and members of their congregations, their congregations probably have little idea of what is going on at the special project. It was their opinion, however, that the general public is much more aware of mental health concepts, and more willing to allow the emotionally disturbed or mentally ill to remain in the community for treatment, than it was ten years ago.

The responses above were elicited by Miss Doris Berryman, a research fellow from the anthropology department of a large neighboring university, who was part of a team working in the Elmont District during the year 1962–63 under a grant (#1–R11–MH–933–1) from the National Institutes of Mental Health. There is probably therefore a degree of objectivity in the responses that might not otherwise have been possible.

The respondents, who represent the school community, the community mental health center, and community leadership and lay people, have in general accepted the project, and in most cases are strong supporters of it. If the hypothesis is accepted that the people of Elmont are probably little different from people in most communities, then it follows that similar projects elsewhere would receive the same kind of acceptance and support.

Professional audiences have, from time to time, questioned the use of non-professionally trained volunteers. But this seemed to pose no problem to most of the professional educators and to the director of the community mental health center, once he had an opportunity to review the results of the Elmont special project and had visited it. The same seems to be true of the scores of professional people who have visited from many sections of the United States and Canada. The assistant to the supervising principal has always used the following approach when explaining to professionals:

Classes for emotionally disturbed children are generally accepted when they are taught by a certified teacher and are provided adequate psychological and psychiatric guidance. In New York State such classes are acceptable to the State Education Department when the ratio of children to teacher does not exceed ten to one. Elmont could have put ten children in a room with a highly qualified teacher presently at the special project full-time, and few professionals would have questioned this since adequate psychological and psychiatric supervision is provided. It is the opinion of the authors, however, that with the kind of children in the Elmont special project only chaos and disorder could have resulted from such a procedure. The highly qualified teacher is there full-time and in constant advisory and supervisory contact with the teacher-moms and the children: the difference lies in the fact that the teacher-in-charge has been given twenty additional pairs of hands, the teacher-moms, to help her in her work. The teachers in the Elmont school district understand this, and it apparently is no threat to them.

Perhaps the real threat, if there is one, lies in the fact that some psychologists and psychiatrists feel that no therapeutic benefits can accrue to children except those accomplished by qualified professionals. The Elmont results belie this belief. While the program is educational, much of therapeutic benefit appears to take place in the children.

One need consider only one statistic to realize that the Elmont approach is no threat to any group with a vested interest in the disturbed child: There are presently about thirteen thousand psychiatrists in the United States, of whom roughly three thousand will work with children. Their skills need somehow to be spread more broadly, or the problem of the disturbed child will continue to grow in numbers and severity. Perhaps the Elmont approach is an acceptable, efficient, economical method whereby that which the skills of the psychiatrist and psychologist are capable of accomplishing with relatively *small* numbers of children can be accomplished, through the educator and the teacher-mom, with *large* numbers of children. If this be a threat, so be it.

One of the most encouraging of the summary responses is the attitude of the professionals, as well as the lay respondents, to institutionalization. All were against it except as a last resort, and more important, most indicated a strong belief in the community's responsibility for these children. Generally, they wanted to see the state government and in some cases the federal government assume more responsibility financially.

It should be emphasized that the cost of the Elmont special project is no greater than the cost of normal education. (See Appendix for a detailed cost analysis.) Most communities can afford this approach. It is important that local communities can do much without resorting to big government, state or federal. In this time when so much is demanded of government, it is refreshing to see a relatively small community resolve a critical problem by mobilizing its own resources. It is perhaps a little oldfashioned, but it represents, in part, a return to local, individual, reliance on self.

It seems apparent, too, that the special project has helped to develop in the district's teachers a greater awareness of, and more skill in dealing with, children's problems. It has had some influence on curriculum. These matters are important,

for they assist the professional to become a little more qualified in the area of human relations.

Finally, there clearly appears the need for a spark plug: a
leader to pull together the needed resources, organize them,
and weld them into a program. It is difficult to believe there is
not one such person in almost every community.

8 Summary and Implications

THERE exists a problem of half a million seriously disturbed children. Little is being done for their habilitation, because generally not enough is known about how to work with them. Programs presently designed to help these children are prohibitively expensive. The nature of the children themselves makes work with them unattractive. Educators, overwhelmed by other problems as well as a lack of resources, and facing a tradition of exclusion of the deviate, have not as yet been as helpful as most of them desire to be.

It has been demonstrated in the Elmont project that resources are at hand in a typical suburban community which, if mobilized, can adequately cope with the problems of most troubled children without resorting to hospital or residential treatment. It has been demonstrated, also, that within the community these children, including some childhood schizophrenics, children with a diagnosis of chronic brain syndrome, and combinations thereof, can be sustained educationally while they develop emotional and impulse controls—so that, in time, they can function at school on their own intellectual level. It has also been demonstrated that by mobilizing existing community resources they can be sustained educationally, and helped emotionally, at a per-pupil cost little greater than the annual per-pupil cost for education of children generally. This cost is considerably less than the cost of custodial institutional care with its inherent problems to both the child and the community.

These demonstrations and cost factors have implications for educators and mental health workers. Educators should recognize that these children are educable and, since they are, are entitled to education within the framework of the existing educational enterprise. There has been a tendency on the part of some educators to exclude children of this type by exemption or referral to some other agency. Their assumption may be that special agencies are in a position to do more for the child. However, experience with the Elmont project raises the question of whether the process of exclusion, which severs the child from his established milieu and creates in the child the need to adapt to a new set of circumstances, doesn't create more problems. This could aggravate the basic condition, which is the child's inability to adapt to his present, familiar environment.

The Elmont project maintains an existing equilibrium for the child, while offering him support, skills, and equipment for functioning more effectively, even though his existing equilibrium may be precarious. It avoids another critical problem of the special facility, which is how to get the child back into a normal community setting when he is ready. Too often, because of this difficulty, children remain in the special setting longer than is appropriate. In the Elmont project the child already is in the normal community setting.

Review of the progress of the children clearly indicates these youngsters make accelerated educational and/or emotional progress in the community and school setting. This may be because they do not have to expend energy adapting to a new setting. The energy expenditure of the professional educator and the psychological and psychiatric supporting personnel is infused into the natural adapting process of the child. It is not dissipated trying to help the child adapt to a new set of circumstances before these efforts can be directed toward his fundamental problem—which is why he would be referred to an agency in the first place.

The Elmont project builds on the existing strengths of the child where he is now, and does not attempt to alter the underlying organic or social pathology. This preserves the basic educational integrity of the program. At the same time it permits the inherent therapeutic aspects of the educational process to make their maximum contribution in an uncluttered manner. It will be noticed that, in addition to the educational progress detailed in the case presentations, social adjustment to peer and family seems to have improved in many of these children.

If these results can be achieved in the existing educational establishment, there is hope for the habilitation of children presently receiving little or no formal education or training. If, in the normal procedures of the school programs, these children and their deficits are identified, is it not the responsibility of the educator to adapt his program to their needs? He already does this for the slow learner, the bright child, the physically handicapped, the retarded, and other groups with special problems.

The Elmont experience would strongly suggest that a proper joint effort on the part of the educator, the psychologist, and the psychiatrist can accomplish more with these children than the establishment of separate, expensive, therapy-oriented educational facilities, or hospitalization.

This does not mean that there are not times in the lives of some children when they need hospitalization instead of education. What seems to happen too often, however, is that the educational enterprise operates unilaterally, while the psychological and psychiatric disciplines operate without adequate communication with, and utilization of, the educators. Any of these children is a total unit and needs a combination of the standard procedures of each of these disciplines. There are standard educational, psychological, and psychiatric procedures: what is needed, and what the Elmont approach seems to do, is to integrate these standard techniques into a cohesive program of identification of the total *needs* of the child and to apply known procedures to the total *development* of the child—while recognizing his integrity as an already partially developed biological and social entity.

Aside from these considerations, the nation must rely on the educational enterprise and the community for the habilitation of these children. At the present rate of training of psychologists and psychiatrists the supply will never be adequate to do the job, even if it could be demonstrated that they *could* do it, given the opportunity. The most skilled personnel are also the most expensive, and it is questionable whether financial resources would be available even if personnel could be trained in adequate numbers.

A further justification for the educational approach is the fact that the public school system is the only social agency large enough to make a significant inroad into the problem. There are public schools in, or adjacent to, all communities. The personnel of the public schools are already trained in the areas of child development and educational psychology of the normal child. They could be oriented effectively to the dynamics of the emotionally disturbed child. What needs to be done is to add to the public school establishment the technical skills of specialists in psychology and psychiatry. This would put the schools in a position to discharge their responsibilities to all children, not just the so-called normal. It makes sense, because it involves building into and onto a mammoth community agency already oriented to children. Regrettably, however, the trend seems to be toward establishment of separate, autonomous structures for the unusual child.

Mobilization of community resources can best be accomplished by the educator because he is already part of the major community instrument for children, the school system. Two factors emerge, however, which are of primary importance. There is needed, first, an aggressive, persuasive, knowledgeable leader to organize the resources into a program. Secondly, there are needed adequate numbers of people to work with the children on an ongoing, sustained basis.

The previous chapter reported interviews with educators in the community, and community religious and civic leaders. Almost without exception, these people credit one educational leader for the mobilization of community resources and the sustained operation of the program. Even allowing for the fact that some of these interviewees may have had a personal bias, it is probably safe to say that there has to be a "spark plug." Someone has to make the effort and assume responsibility and leadership. It may be difficult to locate such a person in many communities, but the potential leaders do exist in most communities: the local superintendent of schools or one of his assistants, a local psychiatrist or psychologist, the administrator of a local mental health facility, a local clergyman, a local political figure or civic leader. Only one person is needed—because within the fabric of any community is the inherent response of people to the needs of children. Communities are made up of families; families have children, and all families want children to be trained and educated. The appeal of children who are ill is tremendous. Most people will respond.

Most persons interviewed in the community were of the opinion that this type of special project is the responsibility of the school. It may be inferred from this finding that continuation and even expansion of the present program in the elementary school district, as well as initiation of special programs at the junior high and high school levels, would probably receive public support. This suggests that a combination of community readiness and special leadership represents the critical factor for bringing such a project into existence, and for its successful continuation.

The interviews with community leaders and others suggest there is a trend toward greater understanding of the needs of emotionally disturbed and mentally ill persons. There seems to be an increased willingness, and maybe desire, to maintain and treat these persons in the community. Perhaps most communities would be willing to support a project for seriously emotionally disturbed children. It would be interesting to explore the response, should someone with strong leadership qualities be introduced into a community to try to develop a similar program. If he were successful, it would tend to validate the tentative conclusion that all that is necessary is community readiness and special leadership successfully to implement similar programs almost anywhere. The Elmont experience suggests that community readiness generally exists. Therefore, what is needed is the development of the special leadership. One of the co-authors will be attempting this, on a grant from the National Institutes of Mental Health, during 1964–65.

In addition to leadership, adequate numbers of people are needed to work with these children on a sustained basis. If it is conceded that the educational process should adapt to the needs of individual children, and if it is conceded that the children of the special project represent the extreme range of variability, then the ideal approach is to develop a system of education and training which represents the extreme of adaptability. Logically, this calls for a one-to-one relationship between teacher and pupil. When the attempt is made to handle these children in groups, the capacity of the teacher to adapt to a child's needs is diluted in direct proportion to the number of children in the group. But no social enterprise other than the family can afford, in a training and educational process, one adult to one child. No social enterprise, including the family, can afford one *trained* professional to one child, even if that number of trained professionals were miraculously available. These things being so, the only resolution possible becomes the use of the volunteer teacher-moms.

The most outstanding aspect of the Elmont project is the one-to-one relationship between the teacher-mom and the child. Almost no professionals or lay people had reservations about the use of the volunteer as long as she received adequate orientation, training, and supervision. This would seem to suggest acceptance of volunteers. The Elmont experience clearly indicates that the volunteer teacher-mom can be a reliable source of motivated, oriented, supervised, conscientious personnel to work with the troubled child.

The identification of the many problems of the children in the Elmont project revealed one outstanding feature. No two children were alike. They each reflected markedly different social histories, personality constellations, and educational difficulties. Frequently the problems of the child appeared to be a by-product of the natural order or disorder of the family. Almost all the families which bred and nurtured these children demonstrated readily identifiable, but not easily alterable, social pathology. The efforts of various professional resources to modify significant family relationships affecting some of these children rarely met with any noticeable success. Some of these families functioned as if their integrity depended upon the preservation of the very pathology identifiable as contributing to the disorganization of their child.

Despite individual differences and specific problems, all the children were hyperactive, distractible, impulse driven, and motivated primarily by internal stimuli frequently unrelated to their external environment. Disabilities extended into nearly every area of motor and perceptual organization. Their performance was unpatterned and unpredictable. This variability was extensively reflected in all psychological and educational testing. Intra- and inter-test variability was the rule. At least seven of the eleven children in the project during the research year demonstrated various neurological stigmata suggestive of diffuse damage to the central nervous system, in addition to other identified psychopathology.

In a critical evaluation of this factor, one might suspect that the intrinsic structure of these children made them particularly vulnerable to an imprinting process by their social milieu, and, ultimately, a direct reflection of its disorder. This might then account for the particular variations of personality and function. But it might also serve partially to account for the unusual successes noted in the project. If these children so readily reflect their immediate environment, they may also mirror the planned introduction of order, control, and learning experiences made meaningful through personal relationships. At the same time, the maintenance of the child within the milieu to which he owes his origin, identity, and existence, eliminates his need to expend his psychic energies to modify and adapt to a new environment. A critical review of before and after psychological testing, and ongoing observations, clearly suggest positive personality changes in almost all the children. This suggests a therapeutic process inherent in this educational procedure, even though its intent was and remained educational at all times.

The original purpose of the Elmont project was to provide an effective educational program for children who could not be contained within the regular classroom setting, and who presented serious educational disabilities. Therapeutic principles were adapted and structured into the educational process. The project was never conceived as having a therapeutic objective beyond introducing the children to meaningful learning experiences. On the basis of achieving educational successes through individualized programing, it was felt that other successes might evolve. Since most of the children did demonstrate educational progress through the individualized programing, it is likely that some of the changes noted in the children can be attributed to their educational successes. However, the inferences of psychological testing suggest more extensive changes taking place. Thus in addition to the educational progress made possible by the methodology of this project there seems to be an inherent therapeutic process, which in turn enhances the educational gains. This factor may account for the sometimes dramatic changes observed in a number of the children.

In examining their psychological and educational records, their extreme variability raises the critical question of the applicability of the group educational process to these children. Order, patterned behavior, relatedness, and some conformity are essential to the successful subsistence of the individual within the group. These are the very ingredients lacking in these children. As a result, their initial educational and group experiences become a series of failures and growing frustrations for both child and teacher. Within the hierarchy of growth and development success breeds success, failure breeds failure. The child's own internal disorganization creates the fabric of failure to clothe his early group experiences, both pre-school and in school. Unaided and left to his own resources within the normal group educational process, failure becomes the established pattern. The child then views failure as a positive gain to be pursued actively, in order to preserve the established pattern of his own identity. He cannot but recognize success in the group educational situation as ego-alien, and, therefore, something to be shunned and avoided.

This may lead ultimately to an anti-educational attitude, which serves to inhibit the child's willingness even to participate in the social-educational system which is a requirement of our culture. It then becomes critical for these children to have their educational patterns properly structured, and geared to a system of success, from the very earliest moments of their exposure. It is conceivable that, in this factor, rests another contributing ingredient to the general success of the Elmont project.

It is possible that the child with psychopathic traits reflects this constellation of personality development in its most intense form. This suggests that the educator, not the psychiatrist, may have the key to the prevention and mitigation of psychopathic and sociopathic tendencies which emerge in some of our young. When children are unaided, and left to their own resources after a pattern of failure has been firmly ingrained, they can only follow their established direction. In order to defend themselves from the experience of repetitive failure, they move more aggressively in the direction of their anti-social behavior. Their failure to fit the demands of the educational system ultimately leads to exclusion. The result becomes further entrenchment of the psychopathy. (Edward was an example of this process.) It should be noted that most of these individuals come to the attention of the psychiatric profession with well established pathology. This makes them reluctant candidates for any voluntary participation in programs designed to introduce change, order, and conformity. It could be speculated that the educator may be in the ideal position to come to grips with this ever growing problem. But he will be unable to make the slightest inroads unless he is given appropriate support from the community and the technical assistance of the behavioral scientists.

Careful identification of the problems of the children revealed that no two presented the same constellation of personality or educational difficulty. This highlights the fact that psychiatric and educational diagnostic terminology, at the present time, simply reflects broad categories of patterned order or disorder—not special or specific pathology, which might then lend itself to uniform management and treatment. One is struck by the insular type of development demonstrated by these children, and the unpredictability of the integration of function that may take place in order for them to achieve some meaningful coalescence into a patterned whole. A review of changes which have taken place in each of the children reveals that progress has occurred without any real predictability as to its pathway. Yet, emerging from the material, is the fact that change does come about in a positive and somewhat consistently accelerated manner. It seems safe to assume that the Elmont project presents a methodology of teaching and training which fosters positive change, appears to accelerate it, and permits the necessary bridges to develop between isolated areas of function whose integration is essential for the learning process. As the child experiences success it becomes a critical force in his life: this possibility must be considered, since the majority of the children demonstrated positive changes in their personality patterns. Yet the project was constructed, and conceived of, as directed toward overcoming the educational and social handicaps of these children in adapting to mass educational procedure.

Careful diagnosis is important, but diagnostic dialogue should not be critical for the educator. The educator certainly should work for early identification of these children, but using only the one criterion: Does the child need the kind of adaptation represented by this kind of project.

Early identification becomes important from another standpoint. The data seem to indicate that accelerated educational progress, and a constructive redirection of detrimental psychological processes, are more apt to occur the earlier the adaptive process is made available.

Growth and development in the young are characterized

by progressive differentiation of function and behavior. As this maturational process unfolds, the interrelationships between developing life and environment become an integral part of the emerging personality structure of the child. These relationships are projected in the behavior patterns and performance of the individual, which may then be accentuated by everyday stresses. There may be a pathology to this sequence. Deviations in biological or psychological maturation, once introduced into the pattern of development, become compounded by the child's consequent repetitive failure. This process is particularly evident in the emotionally disturbed child, who frequently demonstrates poorly integrated biological, psychological, and social maturation. The educator, by introducing experiences beyond the readiness or capacity of the child at a given stage of his development, compounds the distortion. The need for recognizing that personality is based on an orderly process of maturation in all areas of development must be emphasized. Any factor interfering with this orderly process introduces a disturbance of sequence, which may then significantly alter the course of the child's development.

This being so, the technique used in the Elmont project of starting these children on an academic program below their actual achievement levels becomes important. Possibly it exposes the child to an opportunity to develop different learning patterns, redirects academic processes, and reinforces proper learning sequence. This device, however, must be highly selective, and based on the identified psychological constellation of each child. It cannot be generalized.

The one-to-one relationship, consequently, is the sine qua non for the successful adaptation of the educational process to the needs of these children. It permits adaptations and adjustments, and accommodations of scheduling, timing, pacing, programing, and methodology, on a truly individual basis. This individualization serves to eliminate the disordered sequence which has interfered with the learning process. It creates and allows for new patterns for successful educational development. Analysis of the educational progress of the children seems to reinforce this concept. Further, the one-to-one relationship is the only method which can accommodate the unconventional pedagogic techniques required by these youngsters.

If this is so, then volunteers, not specifically trained professionally, are in a unique position to help. They have no preconceived set of standards by which to gauge learning expectancies. Properly oriented by professionals, they are able to establish a relationship based on acceptance of the child where he is now, and unrelated to his identifiable academic deficits and successes. Their lack of sophistication in educational techniques allows them to be receptive to the idea of applying basic pedagogical approaches in a direct, forceful, and un-cluttered manner, thus strengthening the communication inherent in the one-to-one relationship. The absence of the self-image of professional teacher permits the volunteer to experience positive satisfaction from improvement in any area of the child's development, not solely the educational. Professional teachers may become anxious if traditional, measurable academic growth does not take place. The teacher-mom does not have a professional teacher image, and therefore is not affected by this limited measure of children's progress.

The teacher-mom volunteer is in an especially significant position to fill those emotional needs for acceptance and affection which are prerequisite for academic progress. Their ability to secure the trust of the children so they begin to respond is helpful in ego building. Moral support, approval, encouragement, are more readily available than in a classroom, and as a consequence it becomes almost impossible for the children not to relate.

Many children in the project demonstrated significant rises in their intellectual functioning, as well as accelerated academic progress. Greater reality awareness was observed in many. Some of these gains carried over into the home. Some parents reported improvement in the functioning of their child within the family. These changes were of a therapeutic nature, and were made possible by the improved learning process mobilized within the child through the special project. The inclusion of therapeutic principles within what is essentially an educational program therefore, appears to be a sound approach to, and a basic premise for, the habilitation of the troubled child.

The educator, psychologist, and psychiatrist need to get together. If community resources are mobilized, what can evolve would represent true democracy in education. It is not enough to say the purpose of the public schools is to educate all the children of all the people, but to operate so that only those children are included who can fit the traditional mold. The schools are the community. They transmit the culture. The evolution of society from rural to urban culture demands that adequate programs be developed for the education and habilitation of the "different" child. The Elmont project provides a helpful and hopeful demonstration that communities can provide for some of the needs our present culture has imposed on the disturbed child and his parents. As progress is made with these unfortunate children, so also will society move a step closer to becoming, in fact, the family of man.

Appendix

Cost Analysis of the Elmont Project

T H E following is a schedule of costs of operation for the Elmont project for the school year, 1962–1963:

Snacks and Parties	$ 97.44
Insurance	25.10
Teacher-in-Charge (pro-rated)	3,820.00
Music Teacher (pro-rated)	310.50
Psychological Services (pro-rated)	595.50
Psychiatric Services (pro-rated)	700.00
Educational Materials	331.11
Transportation	1,456.00
Total	$7,335.65

Cost to the School District

Total Cost	$7,335.65
Snacks and Insurance	122.54
(Paid by Elmont Kiwanis Club)	
Total Cost to District	$7,213.11
Cost per Pupil	721.31
Transportation per Pupil	145.60
Cost per Pupil Less Transportation	575.71

The per-pupil cost of school operation in the Elmont district for all children during the same school year was $680. For an additional cost of $41.31 per pupil, therefore, it would be possible to operate a program on a one-to-one basis. In examining these figures they appear to be lower than the amount spent on normal pupils by many school districts in the Elmont area. There is no state aid now provided in New York under the newly adopted "Diefendorf" formula, except costs can be included in the total operating costs of the district. Programs for exceptional children are only eligible for state aid using the Diefendorf basic $500 per pupil foundation or shared-cost figure. This means that the state shares in costs up to $500 per pupil, and only in proportion to the amount of taxable real estate value in the district related to the total budget. It is a policy hardly calculated to encourage school districts to do very much about special educational needs.

Another interesting comparison is to relate the $721.31 per-pupil cost to the cost of hospital custodial care, which approximates $1,800 per patient in the state mental hospitals (one figure has it as high as $3,500 per patient). It is obvious that the expenditure at the Elmont project will represent a saving to the citizens of the state if these children can be saved from present or eventual institutional care. Another comparison, made with the cost per pupil in special day schools for emotionally disturbed children, reveals even greater disparity since these costs range upward from $2,500.

Index

203